D0843900

Soccer –
Goalkeeper Training

Thomas Dooley & Christian Titz

Meyer & Meyer Sport

Photo & Illustration Credits:

Cover Photos: imago, © fotolia/Rainer Claus
Cover Design: Sabine Groten
Illustrations: www.easy2coach.net

Translated from the original German by Matt Beadle (CETraining)

British Library Cataloguing in Publication Data
A catalogue record for this book is available from the British Library

Thomas Dooley & Christian Titz
Soccer – Goalkeeper Training
Maidenhead: Meyer & Meyer Sport (UK) Ltd., 2011
ISBN 978-1-84126-306-9

© 2011 by Meyer & Meyer Sport
Aachen, Adelaide, Auckland, Beirut, Budapest, Cairo, Cape Town, Dubai, Graz, Indianapolis,
Maidenhead, Olten (CH), Singapore, Tehran, Toronto
Member of the World
Sport Publishers' Association (WSPA)
www.w-s-p-a.org

Printed and bound by: B.O.S.S Druck und Medien GmbH, Germany
ISBN 978-1-84126-306-9
E-Mail: info@m-m-sports.com
www.m-m-sports.com

Table of Contents

Core Themes of Training/Training Examples

General examples

Table of Contents

Table of Contents

For access to exclusive Easy2Coach animations, see page 23

Goalkeeping has changed a great deal in recent years. A goalkeeper doesn't only have to worry about catching or saving balls anymore – he/she is expected to actively be part of setting up play. The modern goalkeeper is, in a way, a sort of sweeper who should be able to organize the defence and then, when they are in possession, quickly turn defence into offence.

If the opponent is hard to break down, then the goalkeeper serves as a sort of quarterback (distributing passes) and as an extra player when faced with aggressive pressing. The goalkeeper should always be able to adapt him/herself to new situations in games and be able to keep the ball in the game. The goalkeeper should be able to master all of the various passing techniques, including short passing with the instep, long passes struck with the laces, clearances, goal kicks, drop kicks, etc., while at the same time not neglecting traditional goalkeeping skills.

We have attempted to include all of these aspects into this book and we believe that you will find the book to be detailed and that all parts of goalkeeping have been covered. We have used our years of experience, together with those of our many friends and counterparts in the game, to try to make this book as interesting as possible

Enjoy the book and your coaching.

Christian Titz & Thomas Dooley

- Precise, direct passing.
- Tactical understanding and a good anticipation of potential play.
- Coaching of the rearguard (defence).
- Managing the pace of the game (quickly switching defence to offence, slowing down play through holding and controlling the ball, etc.)
- Good positional play and game overview.
- Excellent hand-eye coordination, very good technical ball skills with both feet and hands (cleanly dealing with back passes/passes, starting attacks with clean and quickly played low and high balls; targeted goal kicks, throw-outs or dispatching the ball via drop kick).
- Good control of the penalty area
- Good defence abilities on the line and in one-on-one situations.
- Good ability to jump and run paired with good coordination skills.
- High physical stability
- Physical requirements are above all a recognized height of 1.85 meters and a large reach.

Fundamentally, a modern goalkeeper has to have the skills of a outfield player at his disposal complemented with goalkeeper-specific abilities. The goalkeeper acts a type of sweeper, who is constantly involved in the game, coordinates the other players and intercepts the opponent's passes.

1. **High ball:** When the hands are on the ball, the thumbs meet in the middle of the ball in front of the body and the fingers are spread. The ball should always be caught at the highest point. That means the arms must be stretched. The goalkeeper jumps up with one leg and bends the other (for protection).

2. **Low flat ball:** Align the body behind the ball. The goalkeeper goes down on one knee, puts his hands in front of this knee and catches the ball. Make sure the goalkeeper puts weight on both knees. Always put the knee on the ground where the ball is rolling to.

3. **Low ball to the side:** The goalkeeper falls with a push off to the side. He falls to the right by pushing himelf over his right foot towards the ball. And vice versa to the left. The hands and face provide directional protection. For pike jumps (high jumps to the side) do not bend backwards, rather dive slightly forward. By bending backwards, the shooting angle would increase and consequently the contact area for making saves would also increase, meaning the goalkeeper's reach would diminish. As a basic rule, always try to catch the ball. Every goalkeeper has a strong side where he is better and quicker. As such, you should strive to develop equal abilities on both sides. Simply train more often on the weaker side than on the stronger side to balance your skills.

4. **Mid-height ball below chest height:** Position your body behind the ball and scoop the ball from the bottom up with bent arms; pulling the ball towards the chest. Hold the ball with both hands. If this is not possible, push the ball off to the side with the left hand. Right-handed goalkeepers should reach for the ball with their top hand. In this case, the reach is bigger on the left side, as the arm can be guided forward from behind.

5. **Mid-height ball at chest height:** Position your body behind the ball and position your hands in the catching position as described in high ball.

6. **Catching technique:** The aforementioned 5 catching techniques can easily be practiced with balls rolled or thrown from a short distance.

7. **Leg work:** The goalkeeper always has to move towards the front foot/soccer ball and should not fall backwards. He should learn to focus on the ball until he has it under control. In order to practice leg work, lay a pole down lengthways over which the goalkeeper has to guide his kicking foot, in order to fall to the side towards the ball. In the game situation, in which the goalkeeper's knees are in an upright position, he first stands up with his right leg, and then pushes off with his left. He lays with his torso laterally to the left. He then leans forward with both arms and stands up first with the right leg and then pushes off with his left.

8. **Play opening:** The purpose is to play the ball to his teammates in a way that they don't have any trouble controlling the ball. Also, if possible, when throwing the ball, avoid rolling and bouncing balls. In contrast to outfield players the goalkeeper has more opportunities in opening play. He can throw the ball, roll it, strike it or launch it in different ways (volley, drop kick), or pass it out from the back.

9. **Throwing technique:** When performing a lateral throw out, the arm is stretched back like a javelin thrower, and ball laid in the open hand. The outstretched arm is then powerfully thrown forwards, just missing the ear. The bracing step is important here. When the goalkeeper throws with his right hand, the left leg is forward to the side, and vice versa when throwing with the left hand. You can practice throwing techniques against a net, and afterwards incorporate the throwing action into shooting practice, wherein after a ball

is held, it has to be thrown into one of the goals built on the pitch. When rolling the ball, lay the ball in the palm of the hand, step forward and bend both knees (crouching). If rolling with the left arm, the left foot is the standing foot and placed forward. The right arm is swung backwards and then snapped forward in the direction of the floor. The ball is positioned on the ground. The hand pushes the ball forward and directs it. The torso is slightly bent forward.

10. **Shoot/pass technique:** There are different possibilities to train shooting the ball. With the instep (side-footed shot), full shot (laces), outside of the foot, spin shot, drop kick, volleyed shot from the front or side (scissor kick) shooting technique or with a lob.

11. **Receiving and moving with the ball:** Familiarize yourself with training by receiving the ball and moving with it.

12. **Repetition:** After a maximum of 10 balls, change sides or arm/foot.

13. **Concentration:** The goalkeeper must always keep his concentration, as a goalkeeper's mistake often leads to a goal for the opponent.

14. **Adjustments:** The techniques learned should be tried again and again in shooting practice and types of play. Mistakes must be immediately corrected so that no false movements become automated.

15. **Features of training:** Training should be game based and after a shot on goal a consequence should follow.

16. **Goal distance and formation:** Most goals are scored from a distance between 6 and 13 meters from goal. This should also be reflected in training.

17. **Aspects of good training:**
- Demand accuracy and a high pace (slow training does not lead to long-lasting game appropriate consequences).
- Explaining exercises and the subsequent correction of mistakes must not lead to an information overload. Lack of concentration leads to an increase in mistakes. It's imperative to find the right mixture of correcting mistakes and allowing training to flow.
- Players should learn to observe and be able to use what they observe, just as they should in a game.
- Correct mistakes again and again in order to guard against developing bad habits.
- Address the goalkeeper with both factual clarity and empathy.
- In good groups, the coach can imitate a stressful situation in training, so that players can prepare for stressful situations in games (shouting, criticizing players during training, etc.).
- Demand concentration again and again.
- The coach's appearance (body language, pitch of voice, correctional tips) decides the quality of the training.

Two fundamental aspects must always be considered:
1. What is the arm doing?
2. What are the foot and body positions?

1. The fundamentals

Learning ball and movement techniques with the correct shooting and start timing takes time, should be both isolated and combined with passing practice, and learned to be integrated into various types of play.

Exact kicking and passing techniques are important for both outfield players and for the goalkeeper for a successful soccer game. For the outfield players, good passing technique is a basic requirement for a safe and effective passing game in defence, in fast counterattacks and in different types of offense attacks. The results that a good passing technique can bring vary, but scoring goals is the main purpose of a soccer game.

The goalkeeper's kicking and passing technique can bring success to the team. His pass dictates whether play will build up through the center or on the wings. In his repertoire are short, precise passes to the defenders or the defensive midfielder, as well as long aerial balls to the wingers and now and then to the strikers. His passes follow a clean reception of the ball and dribble, or as a first-time pass. His kicking skills are needed in every type of kick and goal kick. The learning of kicking and passing techniques should thus primarily be learned in connection with a previous take and dribble at the highest speed, with as few touches of the ball as possible after receiving passes from various positions, as happens in typical game scenarios. So indeed it is exactly this type of training that enables a realistic game situation and assigns almost simultaneously challenging and targeted goalkeeper training.

It is fundamentally important that mistakes are corrected throughout goalkeeper training so that no incorrect passing and kicking techniques become automatic.

In the game, different kicking and passing techniques are needed. In order to be able to use these in a game, they must first be learned in training.

Kicking and passing techniques in soccer:
• With the instep (side foot)
• With the laces
• With the outside of the foot
• With the side of the foot

- Curled as a curve or banana ball
- As a drop kick
- As a volley
- As a lob

Methodical tips for learning the fundamentals:
1. Positions the group a few meters away from the coach.
2. Explain the course of actions and slowly point out the movement. First, demonstrate in front of the group. Next, the exercise should be demonstrated so that the players see the actions from behind. (Tip: Some children comprehend exercises easier after observing them from different perspectives.)
3. Start slowly and use both feet in equal measures.
4. The course of actions can be initially learned as a dry exercise, in which the players practice the course of actions without the ball.

2. Explanation of the different shot techniques
In the following chapters, general technical information concering the different kicking techniques will first be detailed. Subsequently the different types of kicking will be presented with their technical requirements and their respective outcomes.

2.1 General information
- The standing leg should be placed 30-40cm laterally from the ball.
- The torso is bent slightly over the ball.
- The foot is swung from top to bottom.

Arm-foot coordination while kicking/passing is identified through the following characteristics:
a) Back lift with the right leg: right arm goes back, left arm to the front
b) Back lift with the left leg: left arm goes back, right to the front.
- For clarification, you can let the players kick the air.
- The focus at the moment is on kicking the ball.
- Due to the high difficulty of fine techniques for the player, with low-level groups (e.g., beginners or children) the ball should be played to them in such a way that they can run to meet it and thus use the power of the ball coming towards them. This means their kicking power increases as does their speed.
- Strength of pass/kick, kick accuracy, shot and start timing are decisive factors for a successful completion of the techniques and proper body position.

2.2 Goal kick techniques (laces)
The tip of the foot points down, the ankle is tensed and the torso is bent slightly over the ball. The contact area is the back of the foot. In order to extend the length of the ball, leaning back slightly is allowed.

2.3 Curling
The ball is kicked with the instep/tip of the foot and receives spin. The player lies on his side on the ground. A slight lay off is not unusual.

2.4 Side foot kick
The ball is played partly with the side foot and partly with the laces. The standing foot is positioned laterally next to the ball and the player's torso tilts forward.

2.5 Side foot shot
The tip of foot points up, the ankle is tensed tightly and angled 90* to the side, the playing foot is slightly raised. The ball has to be met in the middle. Bring the body over the ball and avoid hunching the back.

2.6 Shot with the outside of the foot
When playing the ball with the outside of the foot, a slight lay off is possible, the ball is played with the outer toes and outside of the foot and therefore gets spin.

2.7 Kicking technique – drop kick
When performing a drop kick, the ball is met by the laces at exactly the moment it touches the ground.

Learning aid: drop kick
Take the ball in both hands, stretch the arms out and drop the ball. The ball has to be met by the laces at exactly the moment it touches the ground. The leg follows through after contact. The ball should not spin.

For many children, this technique is very difficult to learn and takes some time for the movements to become automated. It can be helpful to allow the child to kick next to the ball at the moment it hits the ground to develop the right feeling/timing for the correct point of contact without having to keep collecting the ball. It can also help to encourage the point of contact by prompting them when to kick the ball by saying „Now!". It is good to do this in front of a net.

Problems and correctional help when drop kicking:
The ball is kicked too early (before it hits the ground) => demonstrate and explain.
The ball is kicked too late => demonstrate and explain.

2.8 Kicking technique – volley from the front or side (scissor kick) kicking stance
When performing a frontal volley, the torso is bent slightly over the ball. The ball is thrown slightly forward from the hands and met at a low point (not too high). In this way, the ball receives strong pressure and a high degree of accuracy. The area of contact is the laces. In order to gain greater distance, it makes sense to position the torso upright or lean backwards slightly.
When performing a volley from the side, the standing leg is positioned laterally next to the ball and the player's torso is angled. The toes point down, similar to a shot with the laces. The point of contact is the laces, the shooting leg is tilted at an angle and the ball is lightly guided/thrown by the hand to the shooting leg.

2.9 Lobs
When lobbing, the foot goes under the ball, which is then powerfully raised up.

3. Explanation of different throwing techniques
This chapter dedicates itself to two common throwing techniques. The purpose is to accurately throw the ball to a the teammate or to throw the ball where he is moving to.

3.1 Lateral throw

When performing a lateral throw out, the arm is stretched back like a javelin thrower and the ball is laid in the open hand. The out-stretched arm is then powerfully thrown forward, just missing the ear. The bracing step is important here. When the goalkeeper throws with the right hand, the left leg is forward to the side, and vice versa when throwing with the left hand. You can practice throwing techniques against a net, and afterward incorporate the throwing action into shooting practice, where after a ball is held, it has to be thrown into one of the goals built on the field.

3.2 Throwing technique – rolling

When rolling the ball, lay the ball in the palm of the hand, step forward and bend both knees (crouching). If rolling with the left arm, the left foot is the standing foot and placed forward. The right arm is swung backwards and then snapped forward in the direction of the ground. Thus the ball is positioned on the ground. The hand forces the ball forward and directs it. The torso is slightly bent forward.

4. Correctional tips for the coach
- Meet the ball in front of the standing leg
- Follow through after contact with the ball
- The foot points to the ground
- The ankle is tensed
- Pay attention to correct arm positions
- Small steps to the ball
- When making long distance kicks, don't let the ball slide over the laces
- Don't put too much spin on the ball
- Don't play the ball too high, as the longer it is in the air, the harder it is for the receiver to control
- Don't play a banana shot as a goal kick

An almost linear trajectory of 3m in the air is optimal.
When throwing, don't let the ball slide too strongly off the palm. Don't throw the ball too high, as it will be in the air too long. Put as much power behind the ball as possible.
When rolling the ball out, let go of the ball 50cm (at the very least) away from the standing leg.

5. Technique and posture receiving and moving with the ball
- Receiving and moving with the ball should fundamentally ensue after contact with ball.
- Receiving and moving with the ball can occur with the side or outside of the left or right foot.
When receiving high passes/back passes the goalkeeper must bring the ball under control at the moment it touches the ground. If controlled correctly, the ball bounces up off the ground, and so can be played in one touch.
- To counter the ball bouncing up and to ensure a swift ball reception and dribble, a goalkeeper has to command good timing and the right techniques to maneuver the ball.
- In the example of receiving the ball and dribbling with the right instep, the motion sequence happens this way: the goalkeeper has to take the ball with the inside of the foot at the moment that it hits the ground. The leg is swung from right to left in the direction of the ball. Then the foot is lightly guided from top to bottom in the direction of the ball and this prevents the ball from jumping up. Body weight is solely playced on the left standing leg. The body weight is shifted to the right through the hips. (The right shoulder is moved to the back.) The focus is on the ball, and the torso is then moved slightly over the ball.

- When receiving and dribbling with the outside of the foot, the ankle is tilted inside. The lower leg is bent inward at the knee so that the foot movement from top to bottom and left to right in the direction of the ball can occur. The area of contact is the complete outside of the foot.

Variations:

Receiving and carrying the ball behind the standing leg, alongside the left foot. Ball reception technique combines the reception of the ball with an immediate change of direction to the side. This technique takes place with the instep. This takes place with a touch on the ball and is a flowing movement. The foot is then moved in the direction of the oncoming ball. Just before contact, the foot is pulled backwards (slightly slower than the speed of the ball). The ball can now be slowly received and guided with the instep at once.

6. Technique and posture moving with the ball – sole of the foot

In this variation, the toes of the foot that touch the ball are pointed up so that when the ball touches the ground the foot partly covers the ball from above and stops it from bouncing up. The leg with which the ball will be received is thereby moved forwards and bent slightly at the knee. The torso remains upright the elbows remain at the side of the body and are bent at the elbow (similar to the arm positioning when carrying a case of water.) The palms face each other.

The fundamentals

The goalkeeper always stands so that his legs are parallel to each other. In dangerous situations he always moves to the ball and is smooth and dynamic in his movement. If, in order to hold a ball shot at goal, he is forced to jump, he does this to the side and if possible slightly forward. Exceptions are corner kicks, cross kicks and free kicks from the wings, which are between the 6-yard box and the edge of the penalty area. A further exception is when an opponent is directly in front of the goal, jumps over the ball and the goalkeeper has a chance to get his hands on the ball by diving forward. The goalkeeper's initial position is in the middle of the goal. He changes his position depending on the opponent's move (e.g., forward to the side, or if they decide to shoot with their left foot rather than their right). The goalkeeper has to change his position in order to tighten the angle for each foot or shooting position.

Attackers with the ball in the penalty area

- A player is trying to score a goal from the corner of the 6-yard box. The goalkeeper positions himself approximately 1 meter in front of the goal line and about an arm's length away from the near post. The shooter is left with a shooting zone of 3m by 1.5m in the far corner.
- In the 6-yard box, the shooter is left with a shooting zone of 1.2m, and the goalkeeper stands with his arms open.
- When an attacker is dribbling toward the goalkeeper, the goalkeeper should remain upright for as long as possible by initially going to the player quickly but slowing to a distance of around 2-3m, so htat the shooting angle is made decisively smaller. At the same time the attacker will be placed under pressure because by running out to meet him, vital seconds of decision-making time are lost.
- When jumping in one of the corners of the goal, the foot or the tips of the feet, have to point in the direction/corner of the goal in which the goalkeeper jumps.

Attackers with the ball outside the penalty area

- Fundamentally the goalkeeper does not stand on his goal line, but rather in front to shorten the shot angle. If a player comes with the ball into an area 25m from the goal, the goalkeeper has to think about going back to his line, in order to escape the danger of a lob getting the better of him. If a player runs to the side of the goal, the goalkeeper moves to the same side.

Free kick/corner kick/cross kick

- When there is a free kick from a distance of 25 metres, you generally don't position a wall but instead position yourself approximately 1 or 2 steps from the goal, whether the shot angle is in the middle or off to the side.
- In the case of indirect free kicks, the teammate in the wall positioned farthest away from goal should run in the direction of the player making the free kick and try to block the ball. The wall is built in such a way that the tallest players cover the near post and the shortest cover the center of the goal. The goalkeeper positions himself roughly where the players in the middle of the wall are standing.
- Generally the goalkeeper stands on his line and then moves 2-3 steps forward in the direction of the free kick in order to tighten the shooting angle.
- Where there are crosses or corners from free kicks on the wings the goalkeeper positions himself in the center of the goal and 1-2 steps in front of the goal line, with the crosser in his line of vision. Through his lateral positioning, it is possible for him to run forward quickly to the near post. He is also in an opportune position to run to the edge of the 6-yard box or to the far post.

Penalties

- Prior to the shot, the goalkeeper should try to get into a central position, 2.5m in front of the goal line. This reduces the shooter's target area to 2.8 meters either side.

- The goalkeeper stands 2-2.5m in front of the goal line, effectively reducing the height of the goal for the shooter to under 2 meters.

Implementation

The goalkeeper's position has very specific requirements. He has to do his job as goalkeeper as well as the duties of an outfield player (sweeper). His most common actions include catching balls, observing the game, organizing his teammates and restarting play from a static ball (goal kick) or following a back pass.

The tasks in detail

1. Observe, concentrate, give support/tips to teammates and organize the defense.

2. Securely keep hold of easy-to-hold balls and exude calm and authority.

3. Good positional play. Positional play is decisive for all goalkeeping action. The goalkeeper always matches his position with the position of the ball. A good sense of positional play paired with a high level of concentration means a better cognitive ability as well as a better ability to react and anticipate the ball's direction. Coupled with good speed, this means that dangerous situations can often be suppressed early.

4. Good goal kicks/ clearances/ throw outs, a precise and powerful short passing game and long (not too high) balls from open play, an assured first touch and ball control. Safely processing back passes and facilitating an organised build up are the core tasks of any goalkeeper.

5. Good technique/specific goalkeeper technique.

6. On average per game (90 min), stop three (often) to eight (somewhat rarer) dangerous balls.

7. Catch crosses or punch them away (occurs much more often than stopping dangerous shots on goal).

8. Save or parry the second ball or rebound.

9. Take over the tasks of an outfield player (sweeper/last man).

10. Be fast to react.

11. Be a fast sprinter and consequently have strong jumping power available.

12. Have a good game overview and understanding of the game paired with a high level of perception and good tactical understanding.

13. Good condition (basic stamina and powerful endurance and pacing).

14. Be in command of strong physical abilities, which enable you to exude and preserve calm even in dangerous situations.

15. Accomplish position-drawn tactical tasks (e.g., in 4-4-2 formation):

- When your team has the ball, come out only as far halfway in your own half as an additional pass option.
- Inside the penalty zone, traverse the width of the goal to the left and right.
- During build up through the defense, stand deep to be open for passes from the center backs or full backs.
- Organize the team against free kicks and correct the team's tactical errors by giving instructions/assignments.
- Restarting play through throw outs, goal kicks, clearances or passes in open play.
- Should the opponent have possession within 30-35m from goal, the goalkeeper's concentration, tactical skills and observation of the ball increase in importance. The goalkeeper's specific action during close range opposition action are: preventing goals, stopping 1-on-1 situations, catching crosses/free kicks, the alignment of the wall during free kicks and the tightening of the shot angle through correct positional play.

Goalkeeper criteria

Techniques
- Catching
- Punching
- Throwing
- Jumping (explosive)
- Sprinting
- Kicking (techniques of movement of the soccer ball, kick, pass, ball control)

Tactics
- Positional play
- Control of the penalty area
- Coaching (organizing, etc.)
- 1-on-1 situation
- Calculate and evaluate dead ball situations
- Build up play

Physical skills
- Stamina (basic, endurance)
- Pacing
- Anaerobic strength (power)
- Mobility
- General coordination
- Reaction time
- Good anticipation
- Decisiveness

Psychological skills
- Courage
- Motivation and determination
- Ability to remain calm during stressful plays
- Mental stability and good understanding of how to avoid errors (as these often mean a goal conceded)
- High degree of self-confidence

1. **General techniques**
   - Just before the striker contact with the ball, the goalkeeper makes a short jump or takes a short step forward. He expands his arm sideways, bends his knees slightly and stands up to meet the soccer ball. The feet point in the direction of the shooter and are about hip-width apart. The torso leans slightly forward and the eyes are fixed on the ball.
   - The goalkeeper always moves off his front foot. He has to learn to keep his eyes on the ball until he has it under control.
   - The goalkeeper mainly keeps his feet parallel (both feet at the same level).
   - The pushing foot is the foot with which you push off from the ground.
   - When catching the ball, the thumbs meet in the middle of the ball, in front of the body, and the fingers are spread.

2. **Holding drop kicks**
   - Body position: Torso is bent forward, knees bent, body is tense.
   - Hands are held to the side, arms are slightly angled.

3. **Low ball from the front toward the goalkeeper**
   - The body must be brought behind the ball.
   - The goalkeeper goes down on one knee, puts his hands in front of this knee (the arms are close to each other and positioned parallel) to collect the ball. Make sure the goalkeeper puts weight on both knees. Always use the knee closest to the ball and place it on the ground. In addition, while pulling the ball to his body, he can push forward off both feet and falls still facing the game, either forward or backwards.
   - The non-shooting leg is the leg farthest from the ball.
   - When taking defensive action, the goalkeeper must never fall backwards, rather he should always fall forward.
     Alternative: After catching the low played ball, drop forward and roll over the shoulder to the side.

4. **Low, lateral ball**
   - Catch while falling forward.
   - The leg nearest to the ground is bent during descent, or in the process goes up.
     When getting up, quickly use one hand to push yourself up. The other hand is ready to react.
   - The foot or tip of the foot is pointing in the direction of the ball, not to the front.
     The takeoff takes place either with or without an intermediate step. Taking many steps wastes time. When taking off, the bodyweight is on the push-off leg.
   - The goalkeeper falls with momentum to the side. To the right, he uses his momentum over his right foot and laterally pushes off over the soccer ball. To the left, he uses his momentum over the left foot.
   - In this course of movement, the hands and face are directed at the shooter. As a general rule, catch and hold on to the ball.
   - Every goalkeeper has a stronger side where he is better and quicker. This also means that he has a weaker side. This weakness can only be improved by training on both sides, whereby the weaker side is trained more often that the stronger side.
   - **Alternatives:** Lateral shots with restrictions of the shooting angle through two posts (distance of 3m from the far post, angled from the 6-yard box). Stay standing 1-2m in the direction of the shooter, with a distance of an arm's length to the near post. Move forward. React by moving forward, don't fall backwards or open the goal up by going to the ground too early.

5. Sliced shot
a) Sliced shot in the corner
- The goalkeeper quickly moves out of the center of the goal into the corner of the goal, jumps with his arms stretched out above him and catches the ball at the highest point. The jumping leg is stretched, the other leg is bent and tucked into the body.

b) Sliced shot in the center of the goal
- The goalkeeper jumps forward with 1-2 steps towards the ball. He should try to catch the ball as far away from the goal as possible. The goalkeeper jumps with his arms stretched out above him and catches the ball at the highest point. The jumping leg is stretched, the other leg is bent and tucked into the body.

6. Corner ball, free kick, cross or cross from side position
- The goalkeeper stands in the center 1-2m from the goal, facing the ball.
- His legs are parallel to each other and are slightly bent at the knees. The torso is bent slightly forward; the arms are to the side of the goalkeeper and slightly bent at the elbows. (Body position is similar to that of a cowboy just before he pulls his gun from his holster.)
- In order to be able to calculate/estimate the flight of the ball, the goalkeeper reacts first after the ball has been kicked.
- If the ball is not able to be caught, the ball is punched to the side with both hands or if necessary with just one hand.
- To gain momentum, bring the hand/fist (when punching with one hand) forward and up quickly from below and behind.

7. One-on-One situation
- Stand upright for as long as possible, spread your arms and place your legs shoulder width apart. Reduce the shot angle by running out quickly. Slow down just before reaching the attacker and move in a relaxed manner towards the soccer ball.
- Don't spread your legs too wide.

8. Penalty kicks
- The goalkeeper should try to edge off his line by two to three steps before the kick is taken, thus reducing the width of the goal.
- The goalkeeper should stay on his feet as long as possible and observe the posture of the player taking the penalty shot before he decides on a corner.
  Alternative/bluff: He places himself slightly to one side of the goal and tries to confuse the shooter. He can also unsettle the player by moving his arms.

9. Free kick from a distance of 25 meters
- Generally no wall will be placed.
- The goalkeeper positions himself for each shot angle in the middle of the goal off to the side towards the ball.

10. Indirect/direct free kicks from a distance shorter than 25m
- The wall is built in such a way that the tallest players stand in the direction of the near post, and the shortest to the center of the goal.
- The goalkeeper positions himself halfway between the wall and the post farthest away from the ball.
- Generally the goalkeeper stands on his line and then moves 2-3 steps forward in the direction of the free kick in order to tighten the shooting angle.

Easy2Coach Animations

Exclusive:

Since you have purchased this book, you have access to all exercises in digital format on: www.easy2coach.net

In order to visualize all the 4-4-2 systems, free animations are available.

www.easy2coach.net

How does it work:

1. Register for free at **www.easy2coach.net/en/motions**
2. Enter your voucher-code: **MM2010E2Co3DS**
3. Get unlimited access to all animations in this book

Training Target
- Goalkeepers

Training Emphasis
- Juggling techniques

Training Aspects

Skills involved:	Speed of movement with ball, Quick anticipation, Control, Quick decisions, Combining technical skill with movement
Age level:	Any age
Level of play:	Advanced
Type of training:	Individual training, Small group training (2-6 players)
Training structure:	Warm-up, Progression
Purpose:	Improve individual skills
Total number of players:	2 or more players, Single player
Participating players:	Goalie
Training location:	Any
Duration:	1-10 min

Activity:
Goalkeeper moves around with the ball in open space.

Implementation:
The goalkeeper starts by throwing the ball over his head and then juggles the ball switching between left and right fist.

Notes:
- Focus is on the ball (head is tilted backwards slightly).
- Torso is upright.
- Arms are parallel to each other and bent at the elbows. The hand is made into a fist, the palms face each other. The arms point up. Arms now punch the ball (maximum amount of movement is 10-20 cm).
- The goalkeeper moves towards the soccer ball, and depending on the flight path of the ball, he may move slightly laterally, forward or backwards.

Field size:
Any

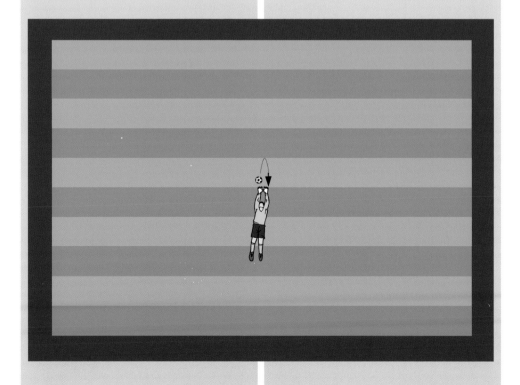

Training Target
- Goalkeepers

Training Emphasis
- Finesse with the ball
- Coordination

Training Aspects

Skills involved:	Speed of movement with ball, Quick anticipation, Control, Quick decisions, Combining technical skill with movement, Quickness of reaction
Age level:	Any age
Level of play:	Advanced
Type of training:	Individual training, Small group training (2-6 players)
Training structure:	Warm-up, Progression
Purpose:	Improve individual skills
Total number of players:	2 or more players, Single player
Participating players:	Goalie
Training location:	Any
Spatial awareness:	Free space
Duration:	1-10 min
Physical skills:	Power & Speed

Activity:
Goalkeeper has the ball.

Implementation:
The goalkeeper stands with his legs shoulder length apart. The ball is taken in both hands and held above the head with outstretched arms. The arms are now moved slightly backwards and the ball is dropped. At the moment the ball leaves his hand, the goalkeeper quickly bends forward (head downwards), reaches behind through his open legs and catches the ball before it hits the ground. Finally he brings the ball back through his open legs and repeats the exercise. Initially the ball can be dropped with outstretched arms at hip height. With beginners, the ball may be allowed to bounce once on the ground.

Notes:
- At the moment the ball is dropped, the body is bent backwards.
- The arms are bent slightly.
- During the movement to catch the ball, the body is bent forward and the back is hunched.
- The arms are approximately 50cm apart.
- During the backwards movement, the player stands on entire foot, and during the forward movement the player moves off the balls of his feet.
- During beginner practices, the arms are stretched backwards and the legs bent at the knees (crouching)

Field size:
Any

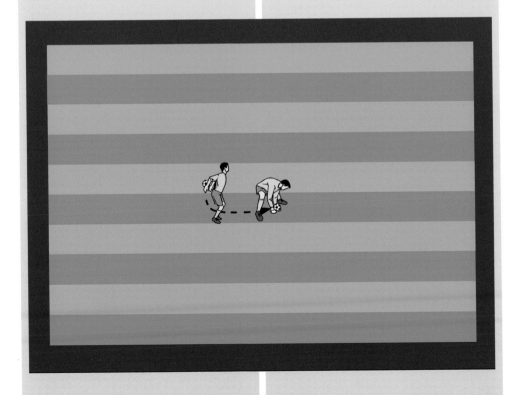

Training Target
- Goalkeepers

Training Emphasis
- Finesse with the ball
- Coordination

Training Aspects

Skills involved:	Speed of movement with ball, Quick anticipation, Control, Flexibility, Speed of movement off the ball, Quick decisions, Combining technical skill with movement, Quickness of reaction
Age level:	Any age
Level of play:	Advanced
Type of training:	Individual training, Small group training (2-6 players)
Training structure:	Warm-up, Progression
Purpose:	Improve individual skills
Total number of players:	2 or more players, Single player
Participating players:	Goalie
Training location:	Any
Duration:	1-10 min
Physical skills:	Power & Speed

Activity:
Goalkeeper has the ball.

Implementation:
The goalkeeper places himself in a wide stance with legs approximately 50-70 cm apart. He bends forward with the ball in his hands and throws the ball sideways and backwards through his legs then he quickly turns and catches it before the ball hits the ground.

Notes:
- At the starting position, the torso is bent forward.
- The legs are bent (crouching position).
- While throwing the ball up, the weight moves slightly onto the balls of the feet.
- After tossing the ball up, the goalkeeper turns in an energetic yet smooth fashion with his torso to the side.
- The turning movement starts in the hips.

Field size:
Any

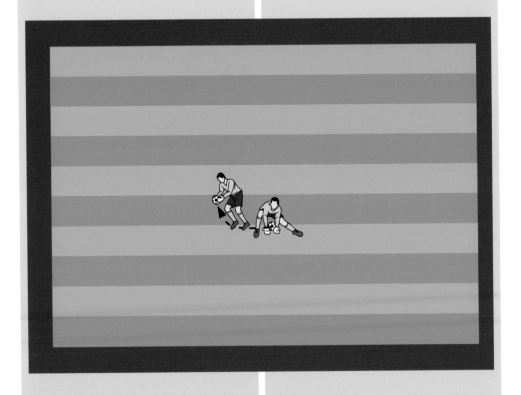

Training Target
- Goalkeepers

Training Emphasis
- Finesse with the ball
- Coordination

Training Aspects

Skills involved:	Leaping strength, Speed of movement with ball, Quick anticipation, Control, Quick decisions, Quick processing, Variable intervals, Combining technical skill with movement, Running technique with/without ball, Quickness of reaction, Quick understanding of danger
Age level:	Any age
Level of play:	Advanced
Type of training:	Individual training, Small group training (2-6 players)
Training structure:	Warm-up, Progression
Purpose:	Improve individual skills
Total number of players:	2 or more players, Single player
Participating players:	Goalie
Training location:	Any
Spatial awareness:	Free space
Duration:	1-10 min
Physical skills:	Power & Speed

Activity:
Goalkeeper has the ball.

Implementation:
The goalkeeper hops and bounces the ball while alternating left and right hands. The hopping should initially be carried out in a forward direction, and later backwards and sideways.

Notes:
- Open palms; do not make a fist.
- Use the balls of the feet, not the whole foot or the heel.
- Tread lightly and loose, do not stomp your feet.
- The arm bent towards the body alternates with the movement of the legs and not away from the body.

- Initially carry out the movements slowly and get quicker bit by bit. A short contact time with the ground and a quick interaction between arms, ball and legs is the goal of this activity.
- While hopping, push up hard with the left leg; the right leg is bent. The left (bent) arm makes an upward movement. The left leg; is almost stretched and pushes off from the ball of the foot. During this jumping movement, the ball is bounced with the right hand towards the left side. When the ball of the right foot hits the ground the same movements begin again with the left leg.
- This exercise demands an enormous amount of coordination. Therefore, the coach should be patient with the player.

Field size:
Any

Training Target
- **Goalkeepers**

Training Emphasis
- **Throw-ins**
- **Finesse with the ball**
- **Coordination**

Training Aspects

Skills involved:	Leaping strength, Speed of movement with ball, Quick anticipation, Quick decisions, Quick processing, Inside of the foot passing Inside of the laces passing, Combining technical skill with movement, Quickness of reaction
Age level:	Any age
Level of play:	Recreational
Type of training:	Individual training, Small group training (2-6 players)
Training structure:	Warm-up, Progression, Main point/Emphasis
Purpose:	Improve individual skills
Total number of players:	2 or more players, Single player
Participating players:	Goalie
Training location:	Any
Spatial awareness:	Penalty box
Duration:	1-10 min
Physical skills:	Soccer-specific endurance, Strength, Power & Speed

Organization:
The goalkeeper stands in the goal. The goalkeeping coach positions himself 12-16m away with balls in front of the goal according to the diagram.

Implementation:
The coach shoots low or mid-height balls toward the goal. The goalkeeper takes the ball with both hands, controls it and at the same time falls forward. Finally, he stands up and rolls the ball back to the coach.

Variation:
Also practice lateral rolls over the shoulder. This is important for game situations with opposition pressure and a forward roll out is not possible.

Notes:
- The goalkeeper always moves off his forefoot. He has to learn to keep focused on the ball until he has it under control.
- He stands with his feet parallel.
- The goalkeeper goes down on one knee, puts his hands in front of this knee (lower arms are close to each other and parallel) and safely collects the ball. Make sure the goalkeeper puts weight on both knees. Always use the knee closest to the ball. Finally while pulling the ball to himself he should push off forward with both feet and fall facing forward and away from the goal.
- When rolling the ball, he places the ball in his palm, the leg closest to the ball steps forward and both legs are bent (crouched position). When rolling with the left arm, the left leg is accordingly placed in front to the right. At the same time, the bodyweight is placed on the left leg. The left arm is guided powerfully forward

toward the ground and thus the ball placed on the ground. The hand thrusts the ball forward and dictates the direction. The right arm makes an exactly opposite backswing movement, parallel to the left hand's rolling movement. The torso is bent slightly forward.

Field size:
Penalty area

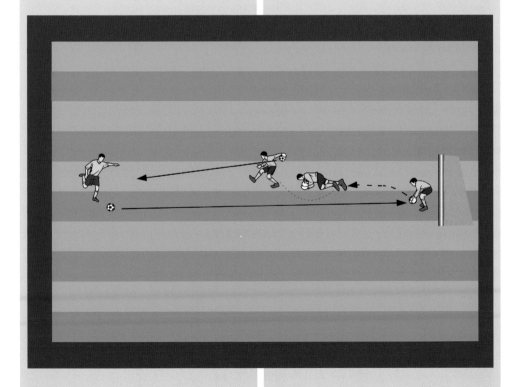

Training Target
- Goalkeepers

Training Emphasis
- Throws
- Coordination

Training Aspects

Skills involved:	Leaping strength, Speed of movement with ball, Quick anticipation, Speed of movement off the ball, Quick decisions, Quick processing, Combining technical skill with movement, Quickness of reaction
Age level:	Any age
Level of play:	Advanced
Type of training:	Individual training, Small group training (2-6 players)
Training structure:	Progression, Main point/Emphasis
Purpose:	Improve individual skills
Total number of players:	2 or more players, Single player
Participating players:	Goalie
Training location:	Any
Spatial awareness:	Free space
Duration:	5-10 min
Physical skills:	Soccer-specific endurance, Strength endurance, Power & Speed

Organization:
Goalkeeping coach and goalkeeper position themselves on the field according to the diagram. The goalkeeper sits 12-16 meters in front of the coach who holds a ball in his hand.

Implementation:
The goalkeeper does a backwards roll, stands up and catches a ball thrown by the coach or fellow goalkeeper. He then makes a lunge forward, throws the ball back, takes a step again and does a forward roll back in the starting position.

Order of movements:
1 Backwards roll
2 Ball thrown by coach
3 Catch ball
4 Ball thrown back
5 Forward roll

Notes:
- The player sits on the floor with bent legs/arms and supports himself on his palms.
- The goalie starts slightly crouched, gains his momentum and roll backwards over his back/head. Here his hands act as levers.
- He lands on his legs and brings himself to an upright position.
- A forward roll follows from a standing crouched movement with a mini-dive forward and finally a roll over the back/bottom.
- During the catching movement the goalkeeper can choose whether he brings the ball to his chest with outstretched arms, or catches it with both palms at his highest point by pushing off with his right leg (rotating with the left).

- During the lateral throw the arm acts like that of a javelin thrower in that it is stretched backwards and the ball lays in the open palm. The outstretched arm is then thrown forward with force, moving just past the ear. The bracing step is important here. If the goalkeeper throws with his right, the left leg is shifted forward, if with the left, the right leg is shifted forward. You can practice this throwing technique against a safety net and afterwards incorporate the throwing actions in shooting practice so that a caught ball has to be thrown into a goal placed as far away as desired.

Field size:
Penalty area

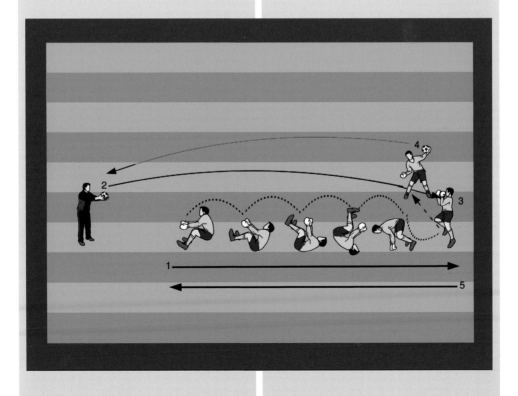

Training Target
- Goalkeepers

Training Emphasis
- Throws
- Finesse with the ball
- Ball control

Training Aspects

Skills involved:	Leaping strength, Speed of movement with ball, Quick anticipation, Control, Quick decisions, Combining technical skill with movement, Quickness of reaction
Age level:	Any age
Level of play:	Beginner, Recreational
Type of training:	Individual training, Small group training (2-6 players)
Training structure:	Warm-up, Progression
Purpose:	Improve individual skills
Total number of players:	2 or more players, Single player
Participating players:	Goalie
Training location:	Any
Spatial awareness:	Penalty box
Duration:	1-10 min

Organization:
Goalkeeping coach and goalkeeper position themselves on the field according to the diagram. The goalkeeper stands 5-8 meters in front of the coach. The coach has the balls. With several goalkeepers, change keepers each round.

Implementation:
The coach throws the balls to the goalkeeper in different ways. Sometimes to the high right of the goalkeeper (1), sometimes directly at knee height (2), sometimes mid-height directly at or to the side of the goalkeeper (3), sometimes high and left of the goalkeeper (4). The goalkeeper has to intercept the balls with different catching techniques and throw the balls back with different one-handed throwing techniques. His arm position varies according to the type of catch or throw:

(1) Catch with one hand high to the right of the body; throw back one-handed with the right hand.
(2) Catch with one hand in front of the body; roll back one-handed, switching between right and left hands.
(3) Catch with one hand in front of the body (for balls thrown to the side, the body has to be brought behind the ball); throw back with one handed over the head.
(4) Catch one-hand high to the left of the body, throw back one handed with the left hand.

In addition to these variations, many other exercises can be incorporated. The ball contact time should reduce with passing time. Ultimately in one short hand movement, the ball is caught and at the same time thrown or rolled back (the catching and returning of the ball is a fast, fluid movement with one ball contact).

Notes:
- The body is, whenever possible with regard to reaction time, always brought behind the ball.
- When catching, the palms are brought behind and slightly under the ball accordingly.
- When waiting for the ball, stand on the balls of the feet and be fast to react.
- Don't allow a long waiting time between exercises. Be sure to repeat often enough to make your actions automatic.
- The precision of the catching movements, the ability to react and a quick switch between defensive and offensive actions will be learned through constant catching and throwing with one hand.

Field size:
Penalty area

Training Target
- Goalkeepers

Training Emphasis
- Finesse with the ball
- Leaping power

Training Aspects

Skills involved:	Leaping strength, Speed of movement with ball, Quick anticipation, Flexibility, Speed of movement off the ball, Quick decisions, Combining technical skill with movement
Age level:	Any age
Level of play:	Beginner, Recreational
Type of training:	Individual training, Small group training (2-6 players)
Training structure:	Warm-up, Progression
Purpose:	Improve individual skills
Total number of players:	2 or more players, Single player
Participating players:	Goalie
Training location:	Any
Spatial awareness:	Penalty box
Duration:	1-10 min
Physical skills:	Soccer-specific endurance, Strength, Power & Speed

Organization:
The goalkeeper coach positions himself according to the diagram, 12-14 meters in front of the goalkeeper. The coach has the balls.

Implementation:
The goalkeeper runs to the coach and catches a ball thrown high. He must catch this at its highest point following a one-legged jump from a running position.

Order of movements:
(1) Set off and run towards the ball
(2) One-legged jump
(3) Catch the ball at its highest point with outstretched arms
(4) Pull the ball towards the chest and land

Notes:
- The ball should be caught at its highest point.
- The arms have to be stretched out.
- The goalkeeper jumps off one leg and bends the other (for protection).
- Pull the ball to the chest as fast as possible.
- Launch off the balls of the feet.
- Take short steps.

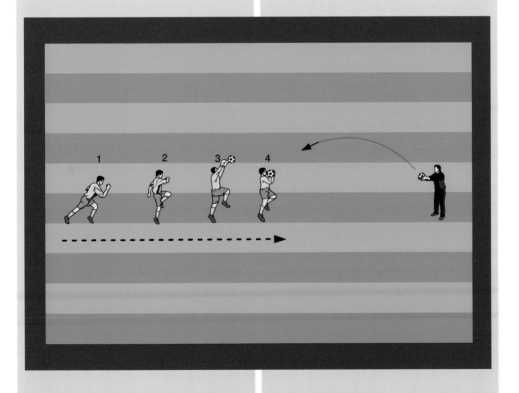

Training Target
- Goalkeepers

Training Emphasis
- Finesse with the ball
- Leaping power

Training Aspects

Skills involved:	Leaping strength, Speed of movement with ball, Quick anticipation, Speed of movement off the ball, Quick decisions, Combining technical skill with movement, Quickness of reaction
Age level:	Any age
Level of play:	Recreational
Type of training:	Individual training, Small group training (2-6 players)
Training structure:	Progression, Main point/Emphasis
Purpose:	Improve individual skills
Total number of players:	2 or more players, Single player
Participating players:	Goalie
Training location:	Any
Spatial awareness:	Penalty box
Duration:	5-15 min
Physical skills:	Strength endurance, Power & Speed

Organization:
The goalkeeper kneels to the side, with the goalkeeper coach standing in front of him in his line of sight at a distance of 5-8 meters. The coach has the balls.

Implementation:
The goalkeeper kneels on the ground with bent arms. The coach uses a backswing to throw; the goalkeeper stands up as quickly as possible and dives towards the flying ball. After he has caught the ball, he throws it back to the coach and the same action is carried out in the other direction.

Notes:
- While the goalkeeper kneels, the torso is in an upright position.
- If the ball flies to his left side, he first stands with his right leg and pushes off with the left.
- In the jump/flight, the goalkeeper tries to make himself as "long" as possible.
- The goalkeeper constantly has the ball in sight.
- The ball should be held tightly with both hands. In case this is not possible, the ball should be pushed off to the side (with the flat of the hand, if he still has to reach for the ball; with the fist when it is played not too far from him). This can be carried out with the hand farthest away from the ground (overlap), or with the hand closest to the ground.
- This variant has the advantage that the reach area is greater.

Training Target
- **Goalkeepers**

Training Emphasis
- **Finesse with the ball**
- **Coordination**

Training Aspects

Skills involved:	Speed of movement with ball, Flexibility, Combining technical skill with movement
Age level:	Any age
Level of play:	Advanced
Type of training:	Individual training, Small group training (2-6 players)
Training structure:	Warm-up, Progression
Purpose:	Improve individual skills
Total number of players:	2 or more players, Single player
Participating players:	Goalie
Training location:	Any
Spatial awareness:	Free space
Duration:	1-10 min

Organization:
Every goalkeeper has a ball.

Implementation:
The goalkeeper holds the ball in his right hand and bends his left leg 90 degrees. He now guides the ball under his bent left leg to his left hand. He then bends his right leg and guides the ball with his left hand under his right leg to his right hand and so forth. The exercise should continue the alternating of sides.

Order of movements:
(1) Start with the right hand, bend the left leg and pass the ball under this leg.
(2) Collect the ball with the left hand.
(3) Bend the right leg and with the left hand pass the ball under this leg.
(4) Collect the ball with the right hand.

Notes:
- Move off the balls of the feet.
- Torso is bent slightly forward.
- Bend the legs at a right angle and pull it high.
- Increase the speed.
- Fluid course of movements.

Field size:
Any

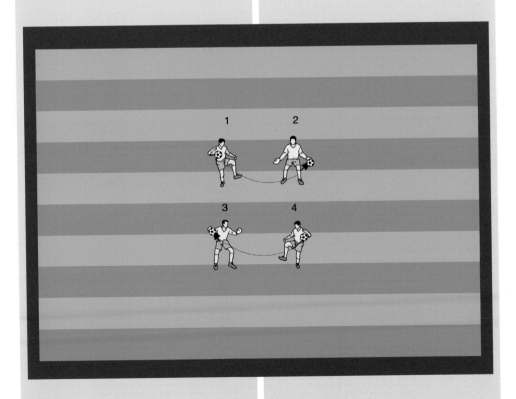

Training Target
- Goalkeepers

Training Emphasis
- Finesse with the ball
- Coordination

Training Aspects

Skills involved:	Speed of movement with ball, Quick anticipation, Combining technical skill with movement
Age level:	Any age
Level of play:	Advanced
Type of training:	Individual training, Small group training (2-6 players)
Training structure:	Warm-up, Progression
Purpose:	Improve individual skills
Total number of players:	2 or more players, Single player
Participating players:	Goalie
Training location:	Any
Spatial awareness:	Free space
Duration:	1-10 min

Organization:
Every goalkeeper has a ball.

Implementation:
The goalkeeper moves the ball around his hips. He starts clockwise with his right hand (1). When he guides the ball past his hip, he moves his pelvis to the left. The change of hands occurs behind his back. The ball is given to the left hand and the hips are pushed forward. Then the ball is again in line with the hips, the pelvis is pushed to the right. The change from left to right hand occurs in front of the body. Here the pelvis is pushed backwards. The drill continues. Eventualy change the direction of movement to counterclokwise (2).

Order of movements:
(1) Clockwise circling of the ball around the hips.
(2) Counterclockwise circling of the ball around the hips.

Notes:
- The coordination of rotating the hips and guiding the ball around the body with the hands is a learning phase for beginners.
- A flowing and increasingly faster movement should be learned.
- The ball is constantly being guided by the hands.
- The torso always remains upright.
- The legs are slightly bent.

Field size:
Any

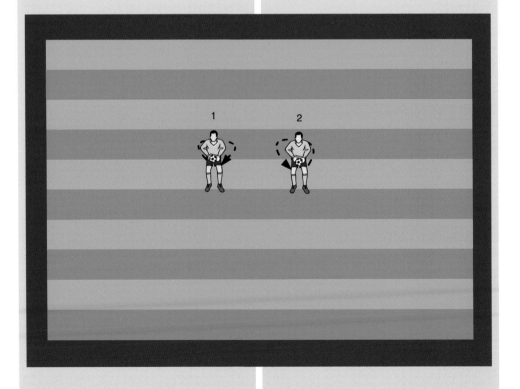

Training Target
- Goalkeepers

Training Emphasis
- Goal kicks
- Throws
- Opening the field

Training Aspects

Skills involved:	Leaping strength, Speed of movement with ball, Quick anticipation, Trapping, Trapping into space, One touch passes, Wall passes, Half-volley, Quick decisions, Quick processing, Inside of the foot, Inside of the foot passing, Inside of the laces passing, Combining technical skill with movement, Short passing, Long passing, Opening the field from the goalie, Volley, Laces
Age level:	Any age
Level of play:	Recreational
Type of training:	Individual training, Group training
Training structure:	Warm-up, Conclusion, Progression, Main point/Emphasis
Purpose:	Improve individual skills
Total number of players:	2 or more players, Single player
Participating players:	Goalie
Training location:	Asphalt, Turf field, Grass field
Spatial awareness:	Free space
Duration:	60-70 min
Physical skills:	Soccer-specific endurance, Strength

Organization:
The goalkeepers move freely with the ball in the training area.

Implementation:
Different passing and throwing exercises are outlined for the goalkeeper. The isolated clearance and throwing techniques can, as described here, be trained in isolation, but they can also be combined with the exercises mentioned above and below. The coach can act as both a passive and active ball distributor.

The exercises illustrated in the diagram are:

1. Clearance technique laces
The front of the foot points down, the ankle is tensed and the torso is bent slightly over the ball. The contact area is behind the back of the foot. In order to obtain greater distance, the ball can be laid off slightly.

2. Curling
The ball is kicked with the instep or front part of the foot and gains spin. The player goes into a lateral position. It is not uncommon for the player to lightly lean back.

3. Kick with the instep
The ball is played partly with the side foot and partly with the laces. The standing leg is positioned to the side next to the ball and the player's torso moves into a slanted position. The toes point down, similar to the foot positioning of the laces shot.

4. Side foot pass
The toes point up, the ankle is tightly tensed and pushed outward at an angle of 90 degrees. The playing foot is lifted slightly. The ball must be played with the middle of the instep. Bring the torso over the ball and avoid hunching your back.

5. Pass with the outside of the foot
When playing the ball with the outside of the foot, lean back slightly if possible. The ball is played with the outer toes and the outside of the foot, and thereby gains spin.

6. Clearance technique drop kick
When performing a drop kick, contact with the ball is made with the laces at exactly the moment it hits the ground.
Tip: Take the ball in both hands, stretch out the arms and drop the ball. The ball has to be met with the laces at the moment it hits

the ground. The leg follows through after contact. The ball should not spin.

7. Clearance technique Volley from frontal position
When performing a frontal volley, the torso is bent slightly forward. The ball is thrown with both hands slightly forward and at a low point. In this way, the ball receives a powerful force and a high degree of accuracy. The contact area is the laces. In order to achieve a long clearing distance, it is advised to straighten the torso up or bend it slightly backwards.

8. Clearance technique volley from lateral position (scissor kick)
When performing a lateral scissor kick, the standing leg is positioned to the side of the ball. The player's torso is slanted. The toes point down, similar to the foot positioning of the laces shot. The contact area is the laces, the kicking leg is diagonally bent and the ball is lightly guided with the hand or thrown to the kicking leg.

9. Lobs
When lobbing, the foot goes under the ball, which is then lifted upward with the laces.

10. Lateral throw-out
When performing a lateral throw-out, the arm is stretched out behind like that of a javelin thrower and the ball is laid in the open palm. The outstretched arm is then powerfully guided forward, which just goes past the ear. The bracing step is important here. When the goalkeeper throws with the right arm, the left leg stands forward. If he throws with the left arm, the right leg is moved forward. You can allow the throwing technique to be practiced against a catching net and later incorporate it into shooting practice, where a caught ball has to be

thrown into a goal positioned as far away as desired.

11. Throwing technique: roll-out

When rolling the ball out, the ball lays in the palm. Step forward with the leg farthest away from the ball and bend both legs (crouching position). If rolling with the left arm, then the right leg should be placed in front of the left. At the same time, the body-weight is put on the right leg. The left arm is powerfully guided forward in the direction of the ground and the ball is then put on the ground. The hand pushes the ball forward and gives it its direction. The right arm parallel to the rolling movement of the left arm, makes a backswing exactly contrary to the movement of the left arm. The torso is bent slightly forward.

Notes:
- The standing leg should be placed 30-40 cm to the side and in line with the ball.
- The torso is slightly bent over the ball.
- The foot is swung from above to below.
- When kicking or passing, the arm-foot coordination is identified through the following characteristics:
  a) Backswing with the right leg: the right arm goes backwards, left arm forward.
  b) Backswing with the left leg. Left arm goes backwards, right arm forward.
- The sight is focused on the ball at the moment of kicking.
- The clearance should not be played as a sliced shot.
- A linear flight path of 3 meters high is optimal.
- When throwing the ball out, don't allow the ball to slide off the hand too powerfully. Don't throw the ball too high, as it will be in motion for too long. Bring as much pressure behind the ball as is possible.
- When rolling the ball out, let go of it approximately 50 cm away from the standing leg at the most.

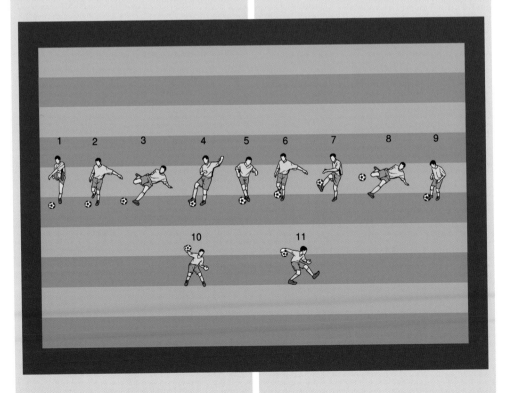

Training Target
- Goalkeepers

Training Emphasis
- Explosiveness
- Reactions
- Shooting

Training Aspects

Skills involved:	Leaping strength, Speed of movement with ball, Quick anticipation, Speed of movement off the ball, Quick decisions, Quickness of reaction, Quick understanding of danger
Age level:	Any age
Level of play:	Recreational
Type of training:	Individual training, Small group training (2-6 players)
Training structure:	Main point/Emphasis
Purpose:	Goalkeeper behaviors, Improve individual skills
Total number of players:	2 or more players, Single player
Participating players:	Goalie
Training location:	Any
Spatial awareness:	Penalty box
Duration:	10-20 min
Physical skills:	Strength endurance, Power & Speed

Organization:
A goalkeeper coach and, if necessary, a another coach, player or goalkeeper positions themselves with the ball inside the penalty area 10 meters away from the goal (see diagram). A goalkeeper is in the goal.

Implementation:
The goalkeeper coach shoots on goal from a narrow angle at different heights mid-height and high balls. The goalkeeper has to parry the balls. After each shot, the goalkeeper has time to reposition himself.

Equipment:
1 full-size goal

Notes:
- The shots should vary in strength (soft/hard) and in alignment (low, mid-height, high, to the body, away from the body).
- The distance of the shots on the goal should not be more than 10 meters.
- Through his positional play, the goalkeeper has to reduce the shooting angle as much as possible. To this end, he positions himself 1-2 m in front of the goal line and has a distance to his near post of approximately an arm's length.
- The goalkeeper tries to catch the ball.
- If the ball is struck too hard or too well placed in the corner, he has to push it off to the side.

- When defending his goal, just before making contact with the ball, the goalkeeper makes a small short jump forward with both legs, spreads his arms out wide, bends his knees, and stands up to the ball. The feet point towards the shooter and are approximately at hip's distance. The torso is leaned slightly forward and the eyes are fixed on the ball.
- When parrying, the goalkeeper must not allow himself to fall forward or backwards, or open up the goal due to a premature dive.

Field size:
Penalty area

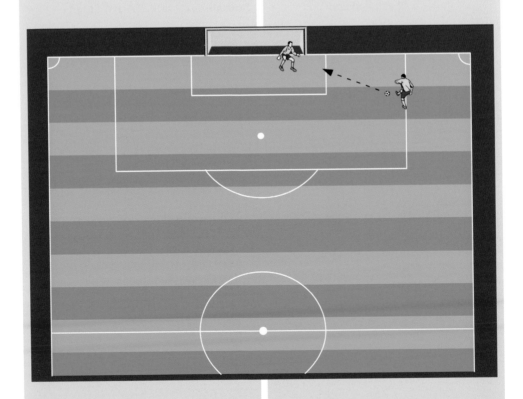

Training Target
- Goalkeepers

Training Emphasis
- Reactions
- Leaping power

Training Aspects

Skills involved:	Leaping strength, Quick anticipation, Flexibility, Speed of movement off the ball, Quick decisions, Quick processing, Quickness of reaction, Quick understanding of danger
Age level:	Any age
Level of play:	Recreational
Type of training:	Individual training, Small group training (2-6 players)
Training structure:	Main point/Emphasis
Purpose:	Goalkeeper behaviors, Improve individual skills
Total number of players:	2 or more players, Single player
Participating players:	Goalie
Training location:	Any
Spatial awareness:	Penalty box
Duration:	10-20 min
Physical skills:	Strength endurance, Power & Speed

Organization:
The goalkeeper is in the goal. The goalkeeping coach positions himself with soccer balls 10-12 meters sideways in front of the goal (see diagram).

Implementation:
The leapfrogging is started in line with the first post. A dive follows after a ball is thrown or shot in the corner of the goal.

Equipment:
1 full-size goal

Notes:
- When jumping, the goalkeeper moves off the front part of his foot or balls of the feet. He has to learn to keep looking at the ball until he has it under control.
- When performing a dive after the ball, the goalkeeper jumps sideways and slightly forward.

- The ball is caught when falling forward.
- The leg closest to the ground bends or moves upward.
- The goalkeeper falls with a step to the side. To the right, by making momentum with his right foot, he pushes off sideways over the soccer ball. To move to the left, he uses his momentum over the left foot. In this movement, the hands and face are directed at the shooter. As a general rule, he holds on to the ball. If this is not possible, the ball should be defended off to the side farthest away from the goal.
- When performing a dive, do not allow the body to fall backwards; rather stretch yourself out in a slightly forward direction. If you fall backwards, the shooting angle will widen and with that the target area for the shooter will increase. That means the goalkeeper's reach will be diminished.
- Dynamic, short, quick movements with short contact time on the ground are key.

Field size:
Penalty area

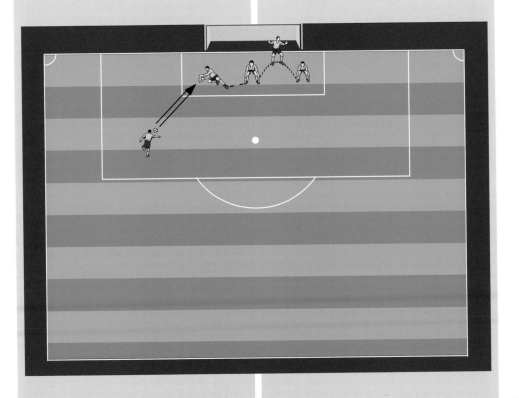

Training Target
- Goalkeepers

Training Emphasis
- Reactions
- Leaping power
- Positional play
- Shooting

Training Aspects

Skills involved:	Leaping strength, Speed of movement with ball, Quick anticipation, Outside of the foot, Flexibility, Speed of movement off the ball, Quick decisions, Inside of the laces passing, Combining technical skill with movement, Quickness of reaction, Laces, Quick understanding of danger
Age level:	Any age
Level of play:	Recreational
Type of training:	Team training
Training structure:	Conclusion, End
Purpose:	Goalkeeper behaviors, Improve individual skills
Total number of players:	8 or more players
Participating players:	Whole team
Training location:	Any
Spatial awareness:	Penalty box
Duration:	5-10 min
Physical skills:	Strength endurance, Power & Speed
Goalkeeper:	1 goalie

Organization:
Every player from the team finds a place on the edge of the penalty area, on which he lays a ball. The goalkeeper is located in the goal.

Implementation:
The players shoot on goal one after another with pauses in-between (the goalkeeper can reposition himself after each shot). The goalkeeper tries to stop the ball.
Shooting competition – team against goalkeeper: Before each round, bets can be agreed upon by the team and the goalkeeper with regard to how many goals will be scored. If fewer goals are scored the team has a fine (e.g., push-ups, carrying equipment back to the changing room, etc.), If more goals are scored, the goalkeeper has to do the agreed upon fine.

Alternatives:
The shooting distance and size of the goal should be suitable for corresponding age groups.

Equipment:
1 full-size goal

Notes:
- The players shoot as soon as the goalkeeper is ready.
- If there are multiple goalkeepers, then the goalkeepers switch after a certain number of shots or after each round.
- The goalkeeper has to reposition himself before each shot according the player's shooting position.

Field size:
30 x 25 m

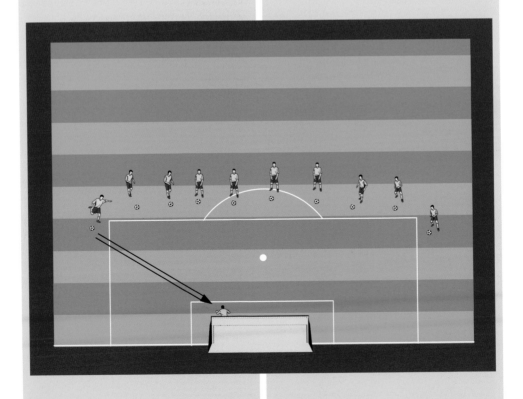

Training Target
- **Goalkeepers**

Training Emphasis
- **Crossing/owning the box**

Training Aspects

Skills involved:	One on one, Leaping strength, Defensive/Offensive play, Speed of movement with ball, Quick anticipation, Speed of movement off the ball, Quick decisions, Bicycle kicks, Wing play without opponents, Running off the ball, Quick processing, Inside of the foot, Inside of the laces passing, Combining technical skill with movement, Heading from a jump, Heading while in motion, Quickness of reaction, Volley, Laces, Quick understanding of danger
Age level:	13-14 years, 15 years to Adult, Under 11, Under 12, Under 13
Level of play:	Advanced
Type of training:	Group training
Training structure:	Main point/Emphasis
Purpose:	Offensive behaviors, Free kicks, Goalkeeper behaviors, Improve individual skills
Total number of players:	6 or more players
Participating players:	Whole team
Training location:	Any
Spatial awareness:	Half-field
Duration:	20-30 min
Physical skills:	Soccer-specific endurance, Power & Speed
Goalkeeper:	1-3 goalies

Organization:
Five players, of which 3 are crossers and 2 are strikers. The goalkeeper is in the goal. The balls are with the crossers. The crossers are positioned approximately 25-30 meters from the goal and the two central attackers are 16 meters from the goal.

Implementation:
The crossers cross balls into the penalty area from differing distances. The two strikers should meet after crossing their runs. The goalkeeper tries to either intercept the crosses directly or to fend off the strikers' efforts. The different positions of the wide players are:
(1) From the touchline
(2) From the mid-position
(3) From the byline

Equipment:
1 full-size goal

Notes:
- The goalkeeper stands facing the crosser.
- He stands in the center, 2-3 m in front of the goal.
- Each time he has to predict whether he can intercept the ball in the air before the strikers arrive to the ball or whether he stays on his line and awaits the strikers' actions.
- If he decides to rush out, he has to try to catch or punch the ball away at its highest point.
- The goalkeeper moves to the direction of the ball from the center of the goal, jumps with arms outstretched above himself and catches the ball at its highest point. The push-off leg is stretched out, the other leg is bent and pulled into the body.

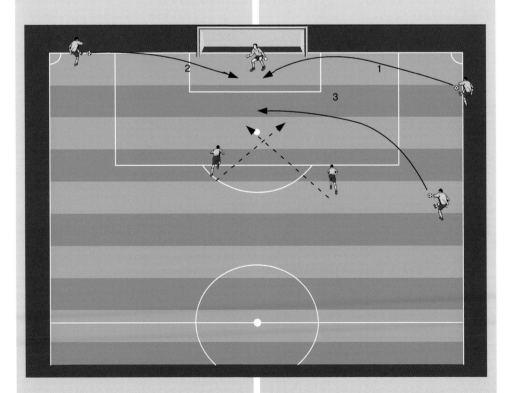

Training Target
- Goalkeepers

Training Emphasis
- **Explosiveness**
- **Reactions**
- **Leaping power**
- **Positional play**

Training Aspects	
Skills involved:	Leaping strength, Speed of movement with ball, Quick anticipation, Speed of movement off the ball, Quick decisions, Quick processing, Combining technical skill with movement, Quickness of reaction, Quick understanding of danger
Age level:	Any age
Level of play:	Recreational
Type of training:	Individual training, Small group training (2-6 players)
Training structure:	Warm-up, Progression, Main point/Emphasis
Purpose:	Goalkeeper behaviors, Improve individual skills
Total number of players:	2 or more players, Single player
Participating players:	Goalie
Training location:	Any
Spatial awareness:	Penalty box
Duration:	10-15 min
Physical skills:	Strength endurance, Power & Speed

Organization:
The goalkeeper is in the goal, the goalkeeping coach is 12-16 meters in front of him with the balls.

Implementation:
The coach throws/kicks balls in the corners. He either kicks a series in one corner or switches each time between the left and right top corners. The goalkeeper tries to stop the balls by diving from the center of the goal (with an extra step if required). Finally he goes back to his starting position.

Equipment:
1 full-size goal

Notes:
- The goalkeeper's starting position is always the center of the goal.
- The goalkeeper begins to move as soon as the ball leaves the coaches' hand or foot.
- The dive may take place with an extra step. Taking many steps means a loss of time. When diving, the bodyweight is on the push-off leg.
- The goalkeeper jumps with a step of momentum to the side. To the right, he uses his momentum over the fight foot and pushes off to the side with the balls of his feet. To the left, he uses his momentum over the left foot.

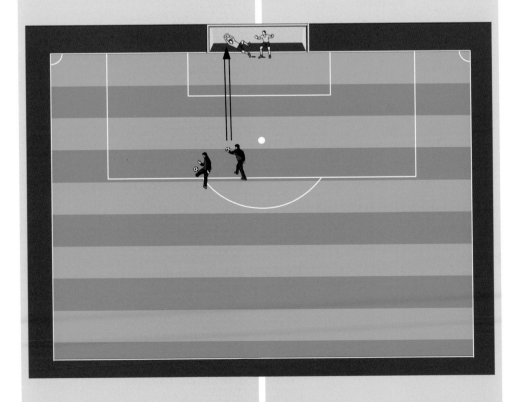

Training Target
- Goalkeepers

Training Emphasis
- Crossing/owning the box
- Leaping power

Training Aspects

Skills involved:	One on one, Leaping strength, Quick anticipation, Control, Speed of movement off the ball, Quick decisions, Quick processing, Quickness of reaction, Quick understanding of danger
Age level:	Any age
Level of play:	Recreational
Type of training:	Individual training, Small group training (2-6 players)
Training structure:	Progression, Main point/Emphasis
Purpose:	Goalkeeper behaviors, Improve individual skills
Total number of players:	2 or more players, Single player
Participating players:	Goalie
Training location:	Indoor, Asphalt, Turf field, Grass field
Spatial awareness:	Penalty box
Duration:	1-10 min
Physical skills:	Soccer-specific endurance, Strength endurance, Power & Speed

Organization:
The goalkeeper stands in front of the goal, and the coach stands to the side of the goalkeeper in line with the penalty area where the balls are.

Implementation:
After jumping from a standing position, the goalkeeper catches the balls thrown by the coach

Variation:
To make it more challenging, a player or other goalkeeper can try to impede the goalkeeper.

Equipment:
1 full-size goal

Notes:
- The goalkeeper jumps forward in the direction of the ball. The arms are outstretched above and the ball is caught at its highest point. The pushing-off leg is stretched out, the other leg is bent and pulled in toward the body.
- To support the take-off, a small hurdle can be placed in front of the goalkeeper.

Field size:
Penalty area

Training Target
- Goalkeepers

Training Emphasis
- **Explosiveness**
- **Reactions**
- **Leaping power**
- **Positional play**

Training Aspects

Skills involved:	Leaping strength, Speed of movement with ball, Quick anticipation, Speed of movement off the ball, Quick decisions, Quick processing, Combining technical skill with movement, Quickness of reaction, Quick understanding of danger
Age level:	6-8 years, 9-12 years, 13-14 years, 15 years to Adult
Level of play:	Advanced
Type of training:	Individual training, Small group training (2-6 players)
Training structure:	Main point/Emphasis
Purpose:	Goalkeeper behaviors, Improve individual skills
Total number of players:	2 or more players, Single player
Participating players:	Goalie
Training location:	Any
Spatial awareness:	Penalty box
Duration:	10-15 min
Physical skills:	Strength endurance, Power & Speed

Organization:
A hurdle is put in the center of the goal. The goalkeeper stands to the side of this. The goalkeeper coach stands approximately 10 meters in front of the goal with the balls (see diagram).

Implementation:
The coach throws the balls so that the goalkeeper has to jump over the hurdle in order to catch the ball. The next phase then starts from the other side so that the goalkeeper switches between having to jump to the left and right.

Equipment:
1 full-size goal

Notes:
- The goalkeeper starts to move as soon as the ball leaves the coach's hand.
- The take-off occurs either without or with an intermediate step. Taking many steps constitutes a loss of time. The bodyweight is on the push-off leg.
- The goalkeeper jumps with a step to the side. To the right, he uses his momentum over the right foot and pushes off to the side with the balls of his feet. To the left, he uses his momentum over the left foot.
- During this activity, the hands and face are facing the coach.
- The aim is to catch the ball without touching the hurdle.

Field size:
Penalty area

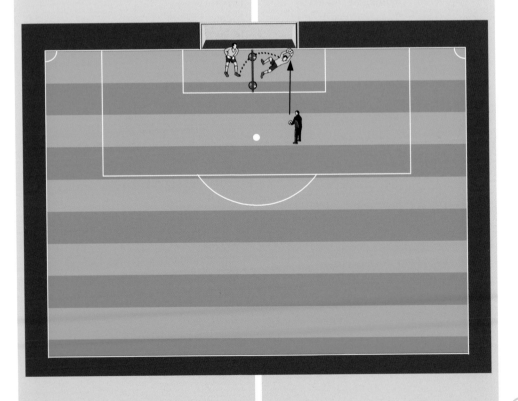

Training Target
- Goalkeepers

Training Emphasis
- Explosiveness
- Reactions
- Leaping power
- Positional play

Training Aspects

Skills involved:	Leaping strength, Speed of movement with ball, Quick anticipation, Speed of movement off the ball, Quick decisions, Quick processing, Combining technical skill with movement, Quickness of reaction, Speed in change of direction, Quick understanding of danger
Age level:	Any age
Level of play:	Recreational
Type of training:	Individual training, Small group training (2-6 players)
Training structure:	Main point/Emphasis
Purpose:	Goalkeeper behaviors, Improve individual skills
Total number of players:	2 or more players, Single player
Participating players:	Goalie
Training location:	Any
Spatial awareness:	Penalty box
Duration:	10-20 min
Physical skills:	Strength endurance, Power & Speed

Organization:
The goalkeeper stands in the goal. The goalkeeper trainer positions himself with the ball in the central position approximately 11 m in front.

Implementation:
The trainer shoots at the goal from a short distance. He varies his shots:
- flat ball in the center/in the corner
- mid-height ball in center/in the corner
- high ball in the center/in the corner
- The goalkeeper tries to keep the ball and after every move returns to the home position in the middle of the goal.

Equipment:
1 full-size goal

Notes:
- The goalkeeper gets into position as soon as the ball leaves the trainer's foot.
- The take-off may take place with either no intermediate steps or just one. Several steps are a waste of time. The bodyweight determines the best take-off with the push-off leg.
- The goalkeeper jumps with force to the side. He slows his momentum over his right foot and shoots sideways to the right with the ball of his foot. To the left, he slows his momentum over his left foot.
- During this activity, his hands and face are the direction of the trainer.
- The purpose is to hold onto the ball or to defend from the side.

- The shot, and the frequency of moves, can be varied. Either have a short break after every shot or after every series of shots (e.g., 3-5 shots= 2-minute break)-

Field size:
16-meter range

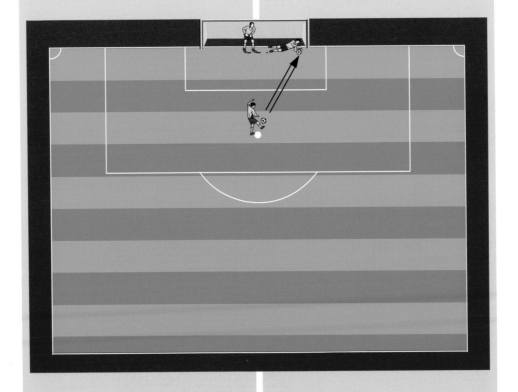

Training Target
- Goalkeepers

Training Emphasis
- Explosiveness
- Reactions
- Leaping power
- Positional play

Training Aspects

Skills involved:	Leaping strength, Speed of movement with ball, Quick anticipation, Speed of movement off the ball, Quick decisions, Quick processing, Combining technical skill with movement, Quickness of reaction, Speed in change of direction, Quick understanding of danger
Age level:	6-8 years, 9-12 years, 13- 14 years, 15 years to Adult
Level of play:	Advanced
Type of training:	Individual training, Small group training (2-6 players)
Training structure:	Main point/Emphasis
Purpose:	Goalkeeper behaviors, Improve individual skills
Total number of players:	2 or more players, Single player
Participating players:	Goalie
Training location:	Any
Spatial awareness:	Penalty box
Duration:	10-20 min
Physical skills:	Soccer-specific endurance, Strength endurance, Power & Speed

Organization:
The goalkeeper stands in the goal. A goalkeeper coach positions himself in a 10-meter range to the side of the goal; the others stand 11 meters from the goal. The goalkeeper coach has the soccer balls.

Implementation:
The goalkeeper coach begins with a shot at an acute angle in the near (goalkeeper) corner. Immediately, the coach, or alternatively a player, throws the second ball into the opposite corner. The goalkeeper must first save the shot and then save the ball that is thrown into the far corner.

Equipment:
1 full-size goal

Notes:
- The shots should vary in strength (easy/hard) and height/alignment (flat, mid-height, and high, on the chest).
- The range of the shots on goal should not add up to more than 10m.
- The goalkeeper should work to reduce the angle through his positional play. In addition, he stays 1-2m in front of the goal line and is approximately an arm's length away from the goalpost nearest the ball.
- The goalkeeper tries to securely catch the ball.
- If the ball is shot too hard or too far into the corner, it must be parried to the side.
- Just before the shot, the goalkeeper makes a small jump with either leg or takes a small step forward (with his arms

out to the sides), bends his legs and stands on the balls of his feet.

- His feet face the direction of the shooter and are roughly shoulder-width apart. The upper body is leaning slightly forward and his eyes are fixed on the ball.
- When saving the ball, the goalkeeper must not dive backwards or leave the goal open by diving early.
- After the move into the close corner, he must try to get to the other corner of the goal as quickly as possible while looking at the goalkeeper coach.
- The ball should be thrown in such a way that the goalkeeper has to jump when running backwards or so that he has to dive sideways into the corner.
- This task can be conducted by both teams.

Field size:
16-meter range

Training Target
- Goalkeepers

Training Emphasis
- Explosiveness
- Reactions
- Leaping power
- Positional play

Training Aspects

Skills involved:	Leaping strength, Speed of movement with ball, Quick anticipation, Speed of movement off the ball, Quick decisions, Quick processing, Combining technical skill with movement, Quickness of reaction, Speed in change of direction, Quick understanding of danger
Age level:	Any age
Level of play:	Advanced
Type of training:	Individual training, Small group training (2-6 players)
Training structure:	Main point/Emphasis
Purpose:	Goalkeeper behaviors, Improve individual skills
Total number of players:	2 or more players, Single player
Participating players:	Goalie
Training location:	Any
Spatial awareness:	Penalty box
Duration:	10-15 min
Physical skills:	Soccer-specific endurance, Strength endurance, Power & Speed

Organization:
The goalkeeper is in the goal. The goalkeeper coach positions himself centrally in line with the penalty area in front of the goal. The goalkeeper coach has the soccer balls.

Implementation:
The goalkeeper runs 7-8 meters out of the goal and then receives a close-range low shot (1). The coach then lobs the second ball to the goalkeeper (2).

A-C: Goalkeeper's path/moves
1: Shot
2: Lob

Equipment:
1 full-size goal

Notes:
- The goalkeeper should stand still for as long as possible, with his arms stretched out and his feet shoulder-width apart.
- To start with, he should run quickly out of the goal then slow down just before he reaches the coach.
- Just before he takes the shot, the goalkeeper makes a small jump with both legs or takes a small step forward, puts his arms out to the side, bends his knees a bit and stands on the balls of his feet. He should point his feet in the direction of the shot and keep them almost hip-width apart, lean slightly forward with his upper body and keep his eyes on the ball.
- After the save, he must immediately be upright again and then run backwards.

- If he fails to catch the ball, the goalkeeper must push with one arm over the crossbar or to the side.

Field size:
16-meter range

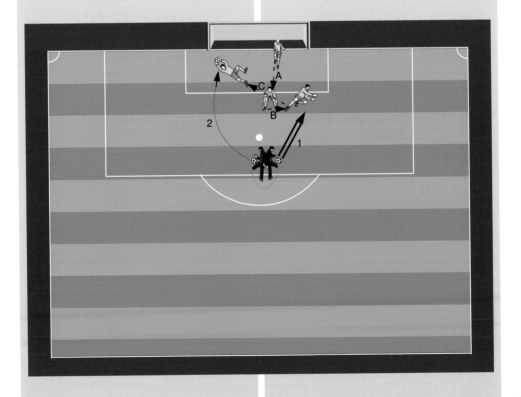

Training Target
- Goalkeepers

Training Emphasis
- Throws
- Explosiveness
- Coordination
- Reactions
- Opening the field
- Leaping power
- Positional play

Training Aspects

Skills involved:	Leaping strength, Speed of movement with ball, Quick anticipation, Control, Speed of movement off the ball, Half-volley, Quick decisions, Quick processing, Inside of the foot passing, Inside of the laces passing, Combining technical skill with movement, Long passing, Positional passing, Quickness of reaction, Speed in change of direction, Opening the field from the goalie, Volley, Laces, Quick understanding of danger, Advanced passing
Age level:	Any age
Level of play:	Recreational
Type of training:	Individual training, Small group training (2-6 players)
Training structure:	Main point/Emphasis
Purpose:	Goalkeeper behaviors, Improve individual skills
Total number of players:	2 or more players, Single player
Participating players:	Goalie
Training location:	Asphalt, Turf field, Grass field
Spatial awareness:	Half-field
Duration:	20-40 min
Physical skills:	Soccer-specific endurance, Strength, Power & Speed

Organization:
Cones/rings/poles/goals are set up. The goalkeepers take their position at the baseline and the coach stands on the penalty spot.

Implementation:
Skipping over poles or jumping through rings while shooting at the goal, the goalkeeper must then play a long ball as a throw-out, punt or a pass on the move into the proper goal.

Equipment:
1 full-size goal, 2 small goals

Notes:
- Pole/ring movement techniques
- Palms showing, don't make a fist. This can account for 3/1000 seconds and can be the difference between gold, silver or bronze for an athlete; in soccer it can determine whether the ball hits the posts or goes in the goal.

- Run on the balls of your feet, don't use your whole foot, just the heel
- Run in an easy, light manner, don't stomp – be light-footed.
- The arms that are bent on the body move the opposite way of the feet. They don't move away from the body.
- Ideally you should move opposite sides of your body (left arm/right foot and vice versa).
- Quick short movements.
- Quick steps=> short, quick movements on the balls of your feet (don't use your whole foot). Your heels must not touch the ground, legs and arms are bent and swing in time with the natural counter-movements (right arm, left leg). The upper body is bent forward. Make little contact with the ground to gain the highest speed.
- Marching => Left foot and left arm are bent. On the ball of the foot, the left foot and left arm are raised. At the same time, position the ball of the foot on the right foot and repeat the same combination of movements. Constantly change your position.
- Knee up run=>Right leg up and bent at the highest angle. Left (bent) arm should be doing the same in an upward movement. Left leg is almost bent. The player stands on the balls of his feet. He positions the ball of his right foot on the ground and follows the same combination of movements as the left foot. His upper body is upright. Make little contact with the ground to gain the highest speed.
- Small jumps/hopping => Left leg pushes up from the ground as high as possible. At the same time, the right leg is bent. The left (bent) arm should be doing the same in an upward movement. The left leg is almost bent and is used to push off

the ground using the balls of the feet. The player positions the ball of his right foot on the ground and begins the same combination of movements as he did with the left leg. His upper body is upright. Making little contact with the ground will give you the highest speed.

Jump technique:
- The goalkeeper must always move on the ball of his foot and step backwards. He should learn to always watch the ball until he has it under control. To practice leg work and quicksteps, lay out a pole lengthways, over which the goalkeeper must move his foot (the foot he uses to push off the ground) to kick the ball sideways.
- In a game situation, in which the goalkeeper is kneeling in an upright position, he first stands with his right leg out and pushes off from the ground with the left. He leans sideways to the left with his upper body, supports himself by putting both arms out in front, stands with his right leg out and pushes off the ground with his left.
- Off-center jumps (skier jumps/moves) => With a slightly forward-leaning torso, alternate between right and left leg, jump forward diagonally (with the right leg, jump diagonally right, with the left, jump diagonally left). It's important that you take off with and land on the balls of your feet. Position the standing leg after the take-off, the other leg is bent (with no contact with the ground) Face forward.

Shooting/throwing techniques:
- The standing leg should be 30-40 cm out and on the same level as the ball.
- The upper body is bent slightly over the ball.

- The arm-foot coordination for shooting/passing has the following features:
  a) Squat jumps with the right leg: right arm goes back, left arm goes forward.
  b) Squat jumps with the left leg: left arm goes back, right arm goes forward.
- Goal kick technique – side foot laces: the forward part of the foot is tense and the upper body is bent slightly over the ball. The ball should be struck with the back part of the instep. To obtain a greater distance, the keeper should slightly lean back.
- Side foot: the ball is sometimes played with a side foot and sometimes with the laces. The standing leg is placed sideways next to the ball and the player's upper body is in a sloped position. The toes point down, similar to the foot position for the instep shot.
- Punting and drop kicks: The ball hits the instep in the exact moment that the ball touches the ground.
- For punting techniques (like frontal volleys), the upper body is bent slightly forward. The ball is thrown forward gently with both hands and hit at a low point. The ball is struck hard and with a high level of accuracy. The ball should be struck with the laces. To reach a better distance, maintain an upright position or lean backwards slightly.
- For punting techniques (like sideways bicycle kicks), the standing leg is positioned next to the ball and the player's upper body is tilted. The toes point down, similar to the position used when making side foot shots. The ball should be struck with the laces, the shooting foot is bent diagonally and the ball is gently guided (or thrown) by hand to the shooting foot.

- For sideways throw-outs, the arm is stretched out backwards like a javelin thrower and the ball is put on flat palms. The stretched arm is then moved close to the ear. The bracing step is important here. If the goalkeeper throws the ball to the right, his left leg shifts diagonally forward. If he throws to the left, the right leg shifts diagonally forward. When rolling the ball, rest the ball on the palm of the player's hand. He goes into the step position with his leg farthest away from the ball placed forward. Both legs are bent (squatting position). Roll your right arm, then place the left leg to the right. At the same time, bodyweight is shifted onto the left leg. The right arm is swung forward in the direction of the ground while the ball is placed on the ground. The hand pushes the ball forward and sets the direction. The left arm goes in the opposite direction of the other arm. The upper body is bent slightly forward.

Field size:
Half a playing field

Distance between cones:
Width: 1 m from the goalpost, 1 m by the
6-yard line
Length: 6 m

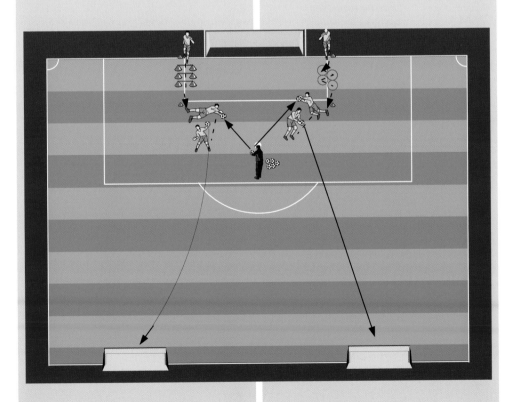

Training Target
- Goalkeepers

Training Emphasis
- Explosiveness
- Reactions
- Leaping power
- Positional play
- Shooting

Training Aspects

Skills involved:	Leaping strength, Speed of movement with ball, Quick anticipation, Outside of the foot, Speed of movement off the ball, Quick decisions, Quick processing, Inside of the foot, Inside of the foot passing, Inside of the laces passing, Combining technical skill with movement, Quickness of reaction, Laces, Taking on multiple players, Advanced passing
Age level:	Any age
Level of play:	Recreational
Type of training:	Group training
Training structure:	Conclusion, Main point/Emphasis, End
Purpose:	Goalkeeper behaviors, Improve individual skills
Total number of players:	5 players or more
Participating players:	Whole team
Training location:	Any
Spatial awareness:	Penalty box
Duration:	10-15 min
Physical skills:	Soccer-specific endurance, Strength, Power & Speed
Goalkeeper:	1-3 goalies

Organization:
The goalkeeper stands in the goal. Several cones are set up at different distances and angles from the goal. The players position themselves in and around the penalty area with the ball at one of the cone markers.

Implementation:
The players take turns shooting at the goal. In doing so, they should use different shooting techniques (curling, laces, instep shot).

Notes:
- The high variability of the shots means the goalkeeper must react differently each time.
- The goalkeeper's purpose is to always secure the ball.
- The goalkeeper reacts as soon as the ball leaves the shooter's foot.
- The jump is made with either no intermediate steps or with just one step. Several steps are a waste of time. The bodyweight moves with the jump made by the push-off leg.

- The goalkeeper jumps to the side with momentum in his step. To the right, he slows down over his right foot and pushes off the ground using the balls of his foot. To the left, he slows over his left foot.

Field size:
25 x 25 m

Distance between the cones:
8-20 m
(This varies according to the age of the group.)

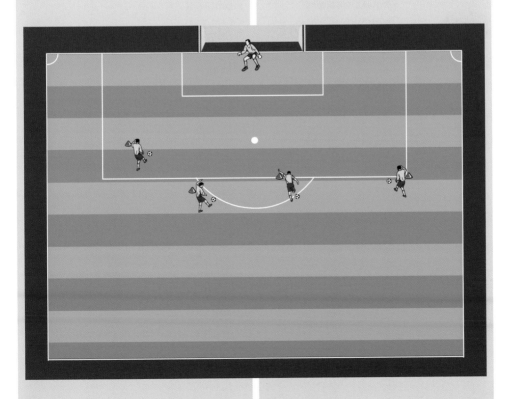

Training Target
- Goalkeepers

Training Emphasis
- Explosiveness
- Reactions

Training Aspects

Skills involved:	Leaping strength, Speed of movement with ball, Quick anticipation, Flexibility, Speed of movement off the ball, Quick decisions, Quick processing, Quickness of reaction, Speed in change of direction, Quick understanding of danger
Age level:	Any age
Level of play:	Recreational
Type of training:	Individual training, Small group training (2-6 players)
Training structure:	Conclusion, Main point/Emphasis
Purpose:	Goalkeeper behaviors, Improve individual skills, Will power training
Total number of players:	2 or more players, Single player
Participating players:	Goalie
Training location:	Any
Spatial awareness:	Penalty box
Duration:	5-10 min
Physical skills:	Strength endurance, Power & Speed

Organization:
Set up a 3-meter-wide cone goal inside the goal. The goalkeeper coach positions himself at a distance of 6 meters in front of the cone goal, in which the goalkeeper is standing. The goalkeeper has the soccer balls.

Implementation:
The goalkeeper coach shoots hard, powerful balls at the cone goal. The goalkeeper must save each ball.

Equipment:
1 full-size goal

Notes:
- Due to the forceful instep close-range shot by the goalkeeper coach the goalkeeper has to react quickly. Therefore, in this exercise the focus is on training quick reactions and overcoming the fear of forceful shots.
- Adjust the forcefulness of the shot according to the age of the goalkeeper.
- Vary the shots between flat, half-height and high balls.
- Feet should point in the direction of the shots and should be roughly hip-width apart. The upper body should lean slightly forward and eyes should be fixed on the ball.
- Balls should be moved to the side.
- After every shot, the goalkeeper must respond immediately to the next ball.
- A series of shots consists of six shots, then a pause of 1-3 minutes.

Field size:
18-yard box (penalty area)

Distance between cones:
From goalpost to cone, 2 m

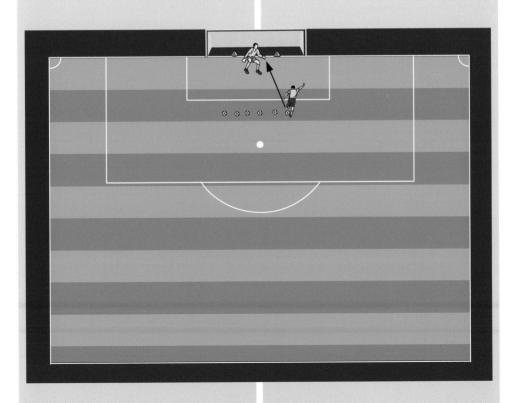

Training Target
- Goalkeepers

Training Emphasis
- **One-on-one**
- **Explosiveness**
- **Reactions**
- **Positional play**

Training Aspects

Skills involved:	One on one, Leaping strength, Defensive/Offensive play, Speed of movement with ball, Quick anticipation, Outside of the foot, Trapping into space, Flexibility, Speed of movement off the ball, Dribbling, Quick decisions, Quick processing, Inside of the foot, Combining technical skill with movement, Body fake, Running technique with/without ball, Quickness of reaction, Laces, Quick understanding of danger
Age level:	Any age
Level of play:	Recreational
Type of training:	Individual training, Small group training (2-6 players)
Training structure:	Main point/Emphasis
Purpose:	Goalkeeper behaviors, Improve individual skills
Total number of players:	2 or more players
Participating players:	Whole team
Training location:	Any
Spatial awareness:	Penalty box
Duration:	5-15 min
Physical skills:	Soccer-specific endurance, Strength endurance, Power & Speed
Goalkeeper:	2-5 goalies

Organization:
The goalkeeper coach or outfield player positions himself with the ball about 16-22 meters away from the goal. The goalkeeper is in the goal.

Implementation:
The goalkeeper coach or outfield player dribbles the ball towards the goalkeeper and tries to outplay him. The goalkeeper must try to prevent a goal and take the ball by skilfully defending the goal.

Equipment:
1 full-size goal

Notes:
- The goalkeeper coach or outfield player should vary his dribbling and speed as often as possible. This means that he dribbles the ball at different speeds and uses different tricks, such as the scissor kick.

Goalkeeper tasks:
- Stay upright for as long as possible, arms spread out and feet shoulder-width apart.
- Reduce the angle for the goalkeeper coach by quickly coming off your line. Reduce your speed or stand still about 2-3 meters in front of the coach and move softly on the balls of your feet.
- Don't spread your legs too far apart.
- The aim is to push the coach or player wide or to take the ball in the moment that it moves too far from the player's feet.

Field size:
25 x 25 m

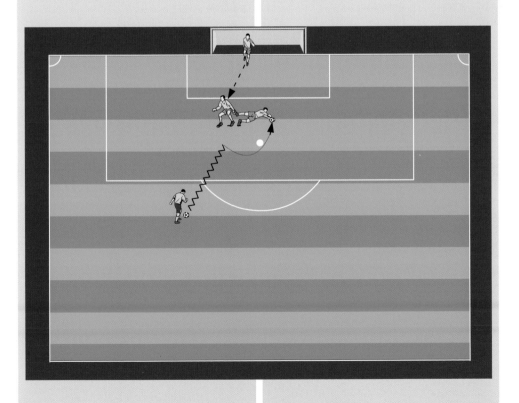

Training Target
- **Goalkeepers**

Training Emphasis
- **Juggling techniques**

Training Aspects

Skills involved:	Speed of movement with ball, Quick anticipation, Control, Quick decisions, Inside of the foot, Combining technical skill with movement, Heading while in motion, Quickness of reaction, Laces, Quick understanding of danger
Age level:	Any age
Level of play:	Recreational
Type of training:	Individual training, Small group training (2-6 players)
Training structure:	Warm-up, Progression
Purpose:	Improve individual skills
Total number of players:	1 player or more
Participating players:	Goalie
Training location:	Any
Spatial awareness:	Free space
Duration:	5-10 min
Physical skills:	Soccer-specific endurance

Organization:
Each goalkeeper has a ball.

Implementation:
The goalkeepers try to juggle the ball. This can be done with all parts of the body except the arms or hands. This can be practiced during recovery as well as during exercise breaks.

Notes:
- When juggling with the feet, you should make sure that you juggle with the instep of both feet (the contact area is the instep, not the toes) This juggling technique is a good drill to learn in order to strengthen and optimize instep shots. The exercise has been done correctly if the ball doesn't spin while being juggled.
- Different juggling varieties or levels of training: right foot- left thigh- left foot- right thigh; right foot- head- left thigh- left foot- head- right thigh- right foot, etc.

Field size:
Any

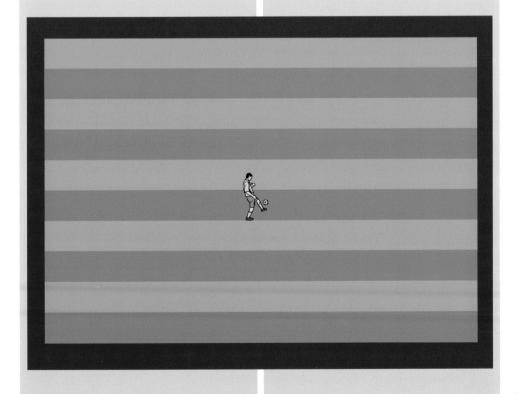

Training Target
- Goalkeepers

Training Emphasis
- Throws
- Opening the field

Training Aspects

Skills involved:	Speed of movement with ball, Quick decisions, Combining technical skill with movement, Opening the field from the goalie
Level of play:	Beginner
Type of training:	Individual training, Small group training (2-6 players)
Training structure:	Warm-up, Main point/Emphasis
Purpose:	Improve individual skills
Total number of players:	2 or more players
Participating players:	Goalie
Training location:	Any
Spatial awareness:	Free space
Duration:	15-20 min
Physical skills:	Strength endurance, Power & Speed

Organization:
The goalkeeper has the soccer balls and medicine balls. The coach stands opposite. The distance (between 10 and 50 meters) to the goalkeepers varies according to shot strength and age group.

Implementation:
The goalkeeper throws the ball, alternating between a regular soccer ball and a medicine ball. He practices the throw outs with his right arm as well as his left. The aim is to throw the balls to the trainer or to the other goalkeepers who are standing opposite him. He should regularly vary his position and distance.

Note:
- Throw outs with the medicine ball is a strengthening task for the arms.
- When doing throw outs, the arm should be stretched out backwards like a javelin thrower and the ball should be placed on an open palm. The extended arm is then brought close to the ear. The bracing step is important here. If the goalkeeper throws to the right, the left leg moves diagonally forward. If he throws to the left, the right leg moves diagonally forward. Throwing techniques can be practiced against a safety net and the throwing technique can be included into training later.
- Throw outs with the ball should be trained at every age level. The use of a medicine ball should not be used with children under the age of 15.

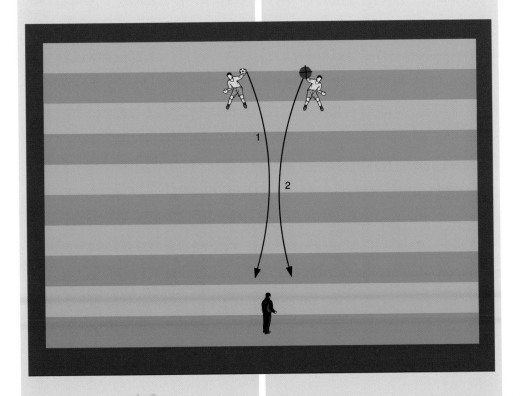

Training Target
- Goalkeepers

Training Emphasis
- Throws
- Passing
- Shot technique/shooting

Training Aspects

Skills involved:	Leaping strength, Speed of movement with ball, Trapping, Half-volley, Quick decisions, Inside of the laces passing, Combining technical skill with movement, Long passing, Positional passing, Opening the field from the goalie, Volley, Laces
Age level:	Any age
Level of play:	Recreational
Type of training:	Group training
Training structure:	Main point/Emphasis
Purpose:	Improve individual skills
Total number of players:	2 players
Participating players:	Goalie
Training location:	Asphalt, Turf field, Grass field
Spatial awareness:	Limited playing field
Duration:	30-45 min
Physical skills:	Soccer-specific endurance, Strength endurance, Power & Speed
Goalkeeper:	2 goalies

Organization:
Each goal has a goalkeeper. The balls are divided up among the goals.

Implementation:
The goalkeepers play against each other using goal kicks and punting on the move or throw outs.

Equipment:
2 goals

Note:
Use punting techniques for drop kicks, frontal volley shots or sideways shots of idle or stationary balls after a pass on the move or a throw out.

Shot and throwing techniques:
- The standing leg should be 30-40 cm to the side and level with the ball.
- The upper body is bent slightly forward over the ball.
- Foot swings from the top down.
- Arm/foot coordination for shots/passes has the following features:
  a) Swinging movement with the right leg: right arm goes back, left arm goes forward
  b) Swinging movement with the left leg: left arm goes back, right arm goes forward
- Goal kick technique for instep shots: the forward section of the foot points down, the ankle is tense and the upper body is bent slightly forward over the ball. The contact point is the back part of the instep. To shoot the ball farther, lean forward slightly.

- Inside/instep shot: the ball is partly played with an inside shot and partly with an instep shot. The standing leg is to the side of the ball and the player's upper body slighly leans forward. Toes point down, similar to the foot's position for instep shots.
- Punting techniques for drop kicks: with drop kicks, the ball is met by the instep of the foot at the exact moment the ball touches the ground.
- With frontal volley punting, the upper body is bent slightly forward. The ball is thrown slightly forward with both hands and met at a low point. The ball obtains speed and accuracy. The contact point is the instep. To reach a longer punting range, stand upright and lean backwards slightly.

- With sideways bicycle-kick punting, the standing leg is next to the ball and the player's upper body is in a leaning position. Toes point down, similar to the foot's position for instep shots. The contact point is the instep. The standing leg is angled and the ball is guided or thrown to the standing leg.
- For side throw outs, the arm is stretched backwards like a javelin thrower and the ball is placed on the palm of the hand. The stretched arm is brought by the ear. If the goalkeeper throws to the right, his left leg moves diagonally forward. If he throws to the left, his right leg moves diagonally forward.

Field size:
Depending on the group's age half or a whole playing field

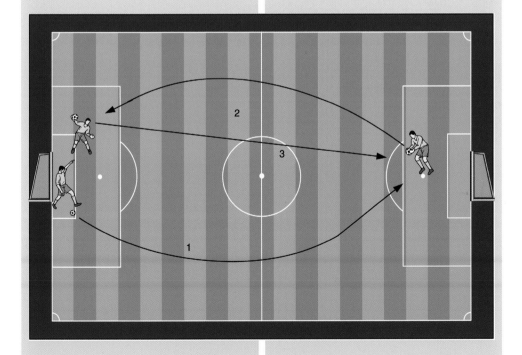

Training Target
- Goalkeepers

Training Emphasis
- Throws
- Explosiveness
- Reactions
- Shot technique/shooting
- Leaping power
- Positional play

Training Aspects

Skills involved:	Leaping strength, Speed of movement with ball, Quick anticipation, Outside of the foot, Trapping, Control, Trapping into space, Flexibility, Speed of movement off the ball, Dribbling, Half-volley, Quick decisions, Quick processing, Inside of the foot, Inside of the laces passing, Combining technical skill with movement, Quickness of reaction, Speed in change of direction, Volley, Laces, Quick understanding of danger
Age level:	Any age
Level of play:	Recreational
Type of training:	Group training
Training structure:	Main point/Emphasis
Purpose:	Training for fun, Goalkeeper behaviors, Improve individual skills
Total number of players:	2 players
Participating players:	Goalie
Training location:	Any
Spatial awareness:	Limited playing field
Duration:	20-40 min
Physical skills:	Power & Speed
Goalkeeper:	2 goalies

Organization:
Set up two opposing goals. One goalkeeper per goal. The balls are distributed among the goals.

Implementation:
The goalkeepers play against each other. They take turns scoring goals in the opposing goal using a variety of shooting and punting techniques. The first to score 10 goals wins

Equipment:
2 goals

Notes:
- Ongoing training of targeted punting, goal kicks, shots on goal or throwing techniques and saves.
- The goalkeeper must constantly be aware of where the shooter is.
- If the opponent shoots from a position far away from the goal, a quick shift to the ball can be advantageous so the goal is not left open.
- Shoot specifically in the corners and watch the goalkeeper. If the goalkeeper stands too far out of the goal, a lob is also a good option.

- Vary the pace of the actions between quick, controlled, preparatory and expectant.
- Correct the positional play, goalkeeper, and shot/throw techniques again and again.
- To increase the fun factor, run several variations in succession.

Field size:
Distance from the goal:
under 14 years old – between 12 and 20 m
over 14 years old – between 20 and 26 m

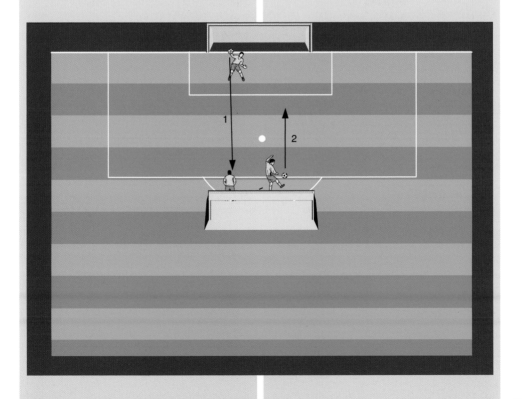

Training Target
• Goalkeepers

Training Emphasis
• **Explosiveness**
• **Reactions**
• **Leaping power**
• **Positional play**

Training Aspects

Skills involved:	Leaping strength, Speed of movement with ball, Quick anticipation, Flexibility, Speed of movement off the ball, Quick decisions, Quick processing, Combining technical skill with movement, Quickness of reaction, Speed in change of direction, Quick understanding of danger
Age level:	Any age
Level of play:	Recreational
Type of training:	Individual training, Small group training (2-6 players)
Training structure:	Main point/Emphasis
Purpose:	Goalkeeper behaviors, Improve individual skills
Total number of players:	2 or more players
Participating players:	Goalie
Training location:	Any
Spatial awareness:	Penalty box
Duration:	10-20 min
Physical skills:	Strength, Power & Speed

Organization:
The goalkeeper coach positions himself roughly 10-22 m away from the goal. A group of people is arranged between him and the goal. The goalkeeper is in the goal and the balls are with the coach.

Implementation:
The goalkeeper coach shoots the balls against the group of people (the wall) at the goal.

Equipment:
1 field goal

Notes:
• As soon as the goalkeeper sees the ball he must respond accordingly and try to save the ball or retain it.
• The goalkeeper's reaction time is delayed by the group of people and he has less time to react to the ball.
• This exercise simulates a deflected shot.
• The goalkeeper coach can shoot the ball in different ways, e.g., a curved shot or an instep shot at the wall.
• If the goalkeeper can't save the ball, he throws it to the side.
• The position of the wall should be changed again and again so that the shooting position and angle are different.
• Depending on where the wall and the shooter meet and the strength of the shot, the trajectory and the speed of the ball will change.

Field size:
Penalty area

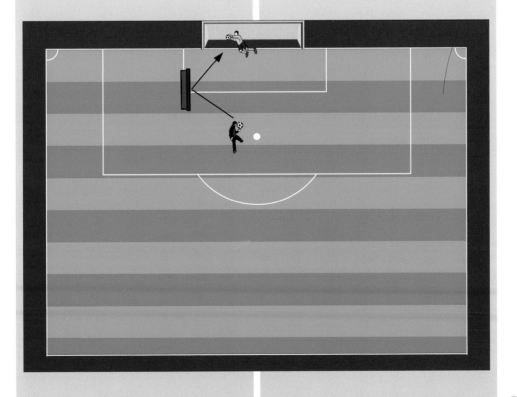

Training Target
- Goalkeepers

Training Emphasis
- **Explosiveness**
- **Reactions**
- **Leaping power**
- **Positional play**

Training Aspects

Skills involved:	Leaping strength, Speed of movement with ball, Quick anticipation, Flexibility, Speed of movement off the ball, Quick decisions, Quick processing, Combining technical skill with movement, Quickness of reaction, Speed in change of direction, Quick understanding of danger
Age level:	Any age
Level of play:	Recreational
Type of training:	Individual training, Small group training (2-6 players)
Training structure:	Conclusion, Main point/Emphasis
Purpose:	Goalkeeper behaviors, Improve individual skills
Total number of players:	2 or more players
Participating players:	Goalie
Training location:	Any
Spatial awareness:	Penalty box
Duration:	10-20 min
Physical skills:	Soccer-specific endurance, Strength, Power & Speed

Organization:
The goalkeeper coach positions himself 14-20 meters in front of the goal. Several cones (preferably round ones) are set up in the penalty area. The goalkeeper stands in the goal and the goalkeeper coach has the balls.

Implementation:
The goalkeeper trainer shoots flat balls at the goal. Depending on whether the ball touches one or more cones, the trajectory of the ball will change. The goalkeeper tries to save the approaching balls.

Equipment:
1 goal, 20 cones

Notes:
- The goalkeeper must react to the trajectory of the ball very quickly. This will help to enhance the player's responsiveness. The goalkeeper should keep hold of the balls as long as possible. If he is unable to hold on, he should discard the ball to the side.
- Just before the coach touches the ball, the goalkeeper does a small jump with both legs or takes a small step forward, spreads his arms out to the side, bends his knees slightly and stands on the balls of his feet.
- His feet should point in the direction of the coach and are about hip-width apart. The upper body is bent slightly forward and the eyes remain fixed on the ball.

- The correct technique for the balls of the feet is very important here. You must be able to push yourself off the ground firmly and at short notice.

Field size:
Penalty area

Placement of cones:
6-10 meters away from the goal

Training Target
- Goalkeepers

Training Emphasis
- **Explosiveness**
- **Reactions**
- **Leaping power**
- **Positional play**

Training Aspects

Skills involved:	Leaping strength, Speed of movement with ball, Quick anticipation, Flexibility, Speed of movement off the ball, Quick decisions, Quick processing, Combining technical skill with movement, Quickness of reaction, Quick understanding of danger
Age level:	Any age
Level of play:	Recreational
Type of training:	Individual training, Small group training (2-6 players)
Training structure:	Main point/Emphasis
Purpose:	Goalkeeper behaviors, Improve individual skills
Total number of players:	2 or more players
Participating players:	Goalie
Training location:	Any
Spatial awareness:	Penalty box
Duration:	10-30 min
Physical skills:	Power & Speed

Organization:
The goalkeeper coach stands with several balls approximately 11-20 meters away from the goal. Roughly 8 meters away from the goal, a barrier, which is a meter off the ground and closed, is set up between the goal and the coach. The goalkeeper stands in the goal.

Implementation:
The goalkeeper coach shoots or throws the balls at the goal. He can shoot or throw the balls under, through, to the side of or over the barrier.

1: Curl the ball over the wall
2: Shoot the ball under the wall
3: Throw the ball over the wall

Equipment:
1 field goal

Notes:
- The goalkeeper will see the ball really late. As a result, his response time is significantly reduced.
- Because of the delay of the ball's arrival into the goalkeeper's field of vision and the delayed awareness of the trajectory, the goalkeeper also has significantly less time to calculate the move and is forced to think and react quicker.
- The goalkeeper's purpose is to hold onto the ball. If he's unable to do this, he should parry the ball to the side.

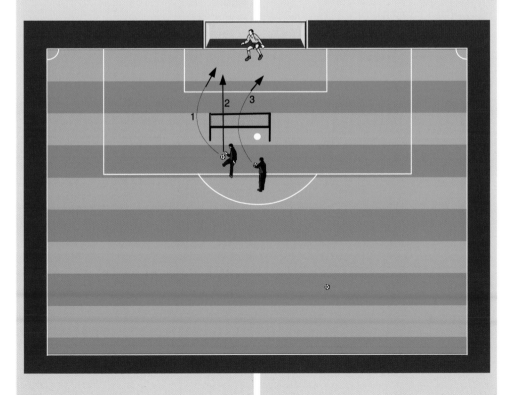

Training Target
- Goalkeepers

Training Emphasis
- Explosiveness
- Coordination
- Leaping power

Training Aspects

Skills involved:	Leaping strength, Speed of movement with ball, Flexibility, Speed of movement off the ball
Age level:	Any age
Level of play:	Recreational
Type of training:	Individual training, Small group training (2-6 players)
Training structure:	Main point/Emphasis
Purpose:	Improve individual skills
Total number of players:	2 or more players, Single player
Participating players:	Goalie
Training location:	Any
Spatial awareness:	Free space
Duration:	5-15 min
Physical skills:	Strength endurance, Power & Speed

Organization:
Several balls are placed at different points on the field. The goalkeeper stands by the balls.

Implementation:
The goalkeeper jumps to ball 1 and controls it, stands up, lets it go and chooses another ball (2), to which he dives, etc.

Notes:
- Jump technique training
- The jump takes place either with no intermediate steps or just one. Several steps are a waste of time. The bodyweight determines the height jump with the push-off leg.
- With a quick step, the goalkeeper falls to the side. He slows over his right foot and pushes off of the ground with the ball of his foot. To the left, he slows over his left foot.
- The leg nearest the ground is bent during the fall.
- When standing up again, use one hand to push off the ground; the other hand is ready to react.

Field size:
Any

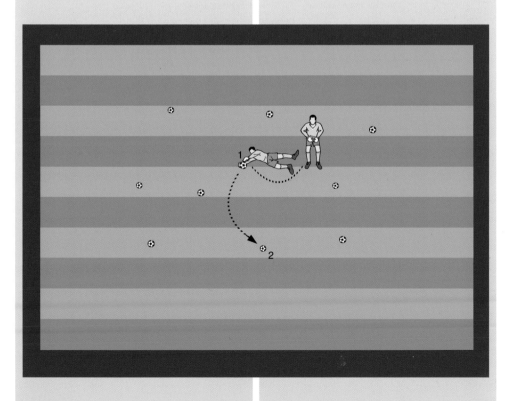

Training Target
- **Goalkeepers**

Training Emphasis
- **Explosiveness**
- **Reactions**
- **Leaping power**

Training Aspects

Skills involved:	Leaping strength, Speed of movement with ball, Quick anticipation, Flexibility, Speed of movement off the ball, Quick decisions, Quick processing, Combining technical skill with movement, Quickness of reaction, Speed in change of direction, Quick understanding of danger
Age level:	Any age
Level of play:	Advanced
Type of training:	Individual training, Small group training (2-6 players)
Training structure:	Main point/Emphasis
Purpose:	Improve individual skills
Total number of players:	2 or more players, Single player
Participating players:	Goalie
Training location:	Any
Spatial awareness:	Free space
Duration:	5-15 min
Physical skills:	Soccer-specific endurance, Strength endurance, Power & Speed

Organization:
Construct a cone course to the side of the goal. The goalkeeper stands at the starting cone (the one farthest from the goal). The goalkeeper coach stands in the middle at a distance of 14-22 meters, depending on the age of the group. The goalkeeper coach has the balls.

Implementation:
The goalkeeper zigzags through the cones. As soon as he has passed the last cone, he makes a 45-degree turn and does a forward roll from the goal. He then receives a shot or throw from the goalkeeper coach.

Combination of movements:
1 - Zigzag
2 - Forward roll
3 - Shot or throw by the trainer

Equipment:
1 field goal, 5 cones

Notes:
- Make quick, short movements through cones.
- The forward roll is done from a stationary crouching position with a mini dive, followed by rolling over the back or bottom. Here the hands and arms act as levers.
- After the forward roll, the goalkeeper must reorient himself immediately. The first ground contact with the feet after the roll prompts the jump after the ball and is a smooth movement.
- Feet point in the direction of the coach and are roughly hip-width apart. The upper body is bent slightly forward and the eyes remain fixed on the ball.
- The purpose is to keep hold of the ball. If the player is unable to do this, the ball should be parried to the side.

Field size:
25 x 20 m

Placement of cones:
Width: 1 m from goal post to first cone
Length: 2 m from goal post to first cone
Between cones: 1-1.5 m

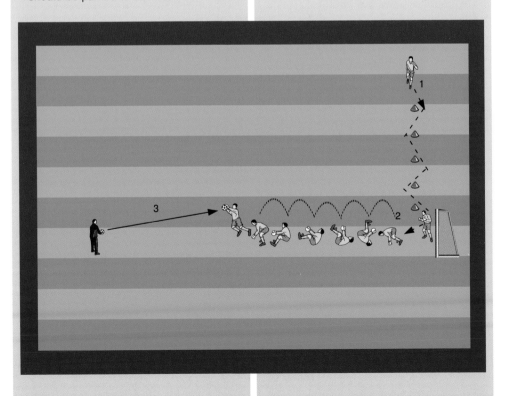

Training Target
- Goalkeepers

Training Emphasis
- Explosiveness
- Reactions
- Leaping power
- Positional play

Training Aspects

Skills involved:	Leaping strength, Speed of movement with ball, Quick anticipation, Speed of movement off the ball, Quick decisions, Quick processing, Quickness of reaction, Quick understanding of danger
Age level:	Any age
Level of play:	Recreational
Type of training:	Individual training, Small group training (2-6 players)
Training structure:	Main point/Emphasis
Purpose:	Improve individual skills
Total number of players:	2 or more players, Single player
Participating players:	Goalie
Training location:	Any
Spatial awareness:	Penalty box
Duration:	10-20 min
Physical skills:	Power & Speed

Organization:
The goalkeeper stands in the goal. The goalkeeper coach stands 11-20 meters in front of the goal with the balls.

Implementation:
The goalkeeper coach shoots several balls at the goal. He can either volley or thrown them.

He continuously varies the speed of the shots and throws, as well as the amount of ground contact the ball has.

Notes:
- Due to the different amount of ground contact and varying speed of the ball, the goalkeeper is forced to keep his eye on the ball.
- Just before the goalkeeper coach touches the ball, the goalkeeper does a small jump with both legs or takes a small step forward, spreads his arms out, bends his knees a little and stands on the balls of his feet. His feet should point in the direction of the coach and are roughly hip-width apart. His upper body is bent slightly forward and his eyes are fixed on the ball.
- Regardless of how the balls approach the goal, the goalkeeper must try to get his body behind the ball.
- The purpose is to keep hold of the ball. If the goalkeeper is unable to do this, the ball should be parried to the side.

Field size:
25 x 25 m

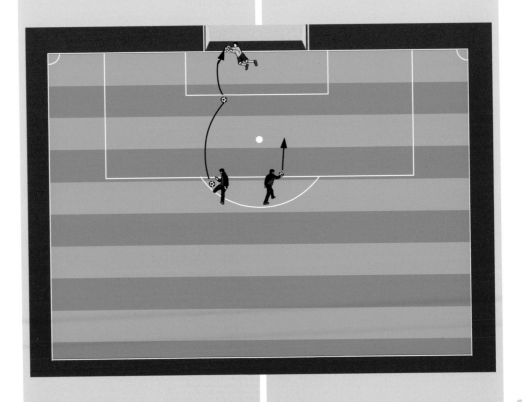

Training Target
- Goalkeepers

Training Emphasis
- Explosiveness
- Reactions
- Speed
- Leaping power

Training Aspects

Skills involved:	Leaping strength, Quick anticipation, Speed of movement off the ball, Quick decisions, Quick processing, Quickness of reaction, Speed in change of direction, Advanced sprint training, Quick understanding of danger
Age level:	Any age
Level of play:	Recreational
Type of training:	Individual training, Small group training (2-6 players)
Training structure:	Main point/Emphasis
Purpose:	Improve individual skills
Total number of players:	2 or more players, Single player
Participating players:	Goalie
Training location:	Any
Spatial awareness:	Penalty box
Duration:	10-20 min
Physical skills:	Soccer-specific endurance, Explosiveness, Speed endurance, Power & Speed

Organization:
A cone is set up on the side of the goal. The goalkeeper stands in the goal, and the goalkeeper coach positions himself, with the balls, 11-16 meters in front of the goal.

Implementation:
The goalkeeper sprints (or runs sideways or backwards) to the cone (1), sprints back to the goal (2) and receives a shot by the goalkeeper coach (3).

Equipment:
1 goal, 1 cone or more

Notes:
- With an explosive start to the cone, stay close to the cone when running around it and run as fast as possible back to the goal line.
- Just before the goalkeeper coach touches the ball, the goalkeeper does a small jump with both legs or takes a small step forward, spreads his arms out, bends his knees a little and stands on the balls of his feet. His feet should point in the direction of the trainer and are roughly hip-width apart. His upper body is bent slightly forward and his eyes are fixed on the ball.
- Regardless of how the balls approach the goal, the goalkeeper must try to get his body behind the ball.
- The purpose is to keep hold of the ball. If the goalkeeper is unable to do this, the ball should be parried to the side.

Field size:
30 x 20 m

Placement of cones:
Width: 5-8 m from goal post
Length: 6 m from goal post

Training Target
- **Goalkeepers**

Training Emphasis
- **Throws**
- **Trapping**
- **Passing**
- **Quick transitioning (defense to offense)**
- **Countering**
- **Opening the field**

Training Aspects

Skills involved:	Leaping strength, Speed of movement with ball, Quick anticipation, Outside of the foot, Trapping, Trapping into space, Flexibility, Speed of movement off the ball, Quick decisions, Quick processing, Inside of the foot, Inside of the foot passing, Inside of the laces passing, Combining technical skill with movement, Short passing, Long passing, Passing over multiple stations, Positional passing, Quickness of reaction, Opening the field from the goalie, Laces, Quick understanding of danger, Advanced passing
Age level:	6-8 years, 9-12 years, 13-14 years, 15 years to Adult
Level of play:	Recreational
Type of training:	Group training
Training structure:	Progression, Main point/Emphasis
Purpose:	Stress training, Improve individual skills
Total number of players:	5 players
Participating players:	Goalie
Training location:	Any
Spatial awareness:	Penalty box
Duration:	15-25 min
Physical skills:	Soccer-specific endurance, Power & Speed

Organization:
The right and left players in the corner of the penalty box have a ball. The goalkeeper is in front of the goal, and the other players are positioned in accordance with the diagram. The pressing player is in line with penalty area, and the other goalkeeper is in line with the half way line.

Implementation:
The left player passes the ball to the goalkeeper. The blue player runs to the goalkeeper and attacks him. He must now decide whether to pass to either the right outside player or to the player on the half-way line, using a direct shot or after receiving the ball. If the goalkeeper makes a long pass to the halfway line, he catches the ball and sends it back to the left outside player using a throw out shot. The training process is repeated alternately from left and right.

Notes:
- The goalkeeper is forced to observe the player's action, and he must be able to react to a pass.
- This will help to train the goalkeeper's attention.

- The goalkeeper must have good control of the ball. The ball control should take place in one touch. The second contact will be a pass.
- The start of play by the goalkeeper takes place from different positions and can be played as a flat pass or a volley.
- For chest control, the goalkeeper should turn in the appropriate direction the moment contact is made with the ball.
- If possible the goalkeeper should pass the ball directly (with just one kick or throw)
- The goalkeeper should use different passing techniques. Volley balls should be played at the front as instep shots.
- The players change their positions regularly, moving clockwise.

- Accuracy and control when passing and during throw outs is required.

Field size:
Half a playing field

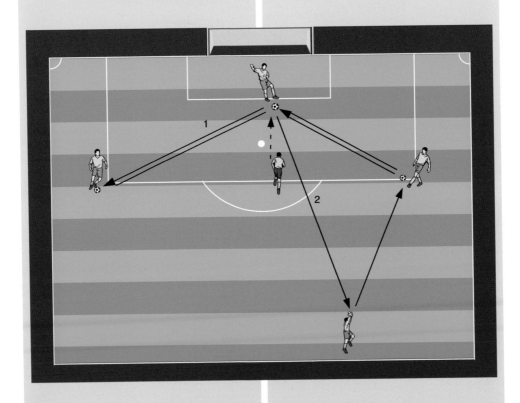

Training Target
- Goalkeepers

Training Emphasis
- Reactions
- Leaping power

Training Aspects

Skills involved:	Leaping strength, Speed of movement with ball, Quick anticipation, Trapping into space, Flexibility, Speed of movement off the ball, Quick decisions, Quick processing, Combining technical skill with movement, Quick understanding of danger
Age level:	Any age
Level of play:	Recreational
Type of training:	Individual training, Small group training (2-6 players)
Training structure:	Warm-up, Progression
Purpose:	Improve individual skills
Total number of players:	2 or more players, Single player
Participating players:	Goalie
Training location:	Any
Spatial awareness:	Free space
Duration:	5 min
Physical skills:	Strength endurance, Power & Speed

Organization:
Each goalkeeper has a ball.

Implementation:
The goalkeeper moves around in free space. While doing so, he constantly throws the ball up and catches it again.

Notes:
- The goalkeeper jumps up and forward in the direction of the ball. He jumps up with outstretched arms and catches the ball at the highest point.
- The take-off leg is extended; the other leg is bent and drawn towards the body.
- The player should not throw the ball too high or too far to the side.
- The player should keep the ball within his field of vision.

Field size:
Any

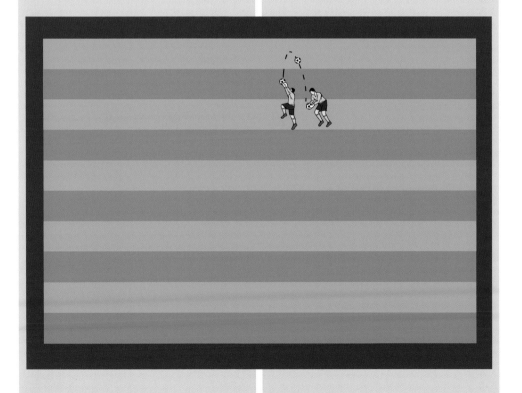

Training Target

- Goalkeepers

Training Emphasis

- Finesse with the ball
- Coordination

Training Aspects

Skills involved:	Speed of movement with ball, Control, Flexibility, Quick decisions, Combining technical skill with movement
Age level:	Any age
Level of play:	Recreational
Type of training:	Individual training, Small group training (2-6 players)
Training structure:	Warm-up, Progression
Purpose:	Improve individual skills
Total number of players:	2 or more players, Single player
Participating players:	Goalie
Training location:	Any
Spatial awareness:	Free space
Duration:	1 min

Organization:
Each goalkeeper has a ball

Implementation:
The goalkeeper makes a figure 8 with the ball through his legs.

Notes:
- The goalkeeper's legs should remain shoulder-width apart. Knees are bent slightly and the upper body is bent forward. The player should hold the ball in one hand and guide the ball through his legs, making a figure 8.
- Start slowly and get faster bit by bit.

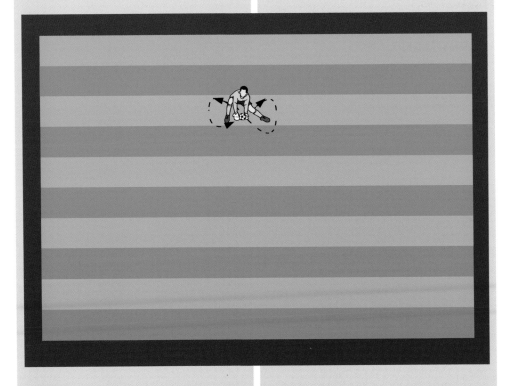

Training Target
- Goalkeepers

Training Emphasis
- Finesse with the ball
- Coordination

Training Aspects

Skills involved:	Speed of movement with ball, Quick anticipation, Control, Flexibility, Speed of movement off the ball, Quick decisions, Combining technical skill with movement
Age level:	Any age
Level of play:	Recreational
Type of training:	Individual training, Small group training (2-6 players)
Training structure:	Warm-up, Progression
Purpose:	Improve individual skills
Total number of players:	2 or more players, Single player
Participating players:	Goalie
Training location:	Any
Spatial awareness:	Free space
Duration:	2 min

Organization:
Each goalkeeper has a ball.

Implementation:
The ball is held between the legs with both hands. One arm grips the ball from behind and the other from in front. Now the player releases the ball and must turn the other way to catch the ball in the same way while bending forward.

Notes:
- The goalkeeper's shoulders should be shoulder-width apart. His legs should be slightly bent and his upper body bent slightly forward. He should hold the ball in one hand, throw it up gently (about 20-30 cm) and turn the other way really quickly to catch the ball again (alternatively the hands grip the left and right leg).
- Start slowly and get faster bit by bit.

Field size:
Any

Training Target
- Goalkeepers

Training Emphasis
- Explosiveness
- Reactions
- Leaping power

Training Aspects	
Skills involved:	Leaping strength, Speed of movement with ball, Quick anticipation, Flexibility, Speed of movement off the ball, Quick decisions, Quick processing, Quick understanding of danger
Age level:	Any age
Level of play:	Recreational
Type of training:	Individual training, Small group training (2-6 players)
Training structure:	Main point/Emphasis
Purpose:	Improve individual skills
Total number of players:	2 or more players, Single player
Participating players:	Goalie
Training location:	Any
Spatial awareness:	Free space
Duration:	5-10 min
Physical skills:	Strength endurance, Power & Speed

Organization:
The goalkeeper coach and the goalkeeper stand opposite each other, 3-5 m apart. The coach has a ball in each hand.

Implementation:
The goalkeeper coach throws the ball in the direction of the goalkeeper, so that he must jump forward, left, right or backwards (depending on the direction of the throw), to catch the ball. The goalkeeper throws the caught ball from the ground back to the coach; he stands up and immediately gets the next thrown ball.

Notes:
- Above all, this task helps to train timing and power of jumps, as well as jumping and catching techniques.
- The goalkeeper starts the move as soon as the ball leaves the coach's hand.
- He either jumps forward or to the side.
- The bodyweight determines the height of the jump off the take-off leg.
- The goalkeeper jumps with force to the side or forward. Jumping right, he slows over his right foot and pushes off the ground with the ball of his foot. To the left, he slows over his left foot.
- During this combination of movements, the player's face and hands face the coach.

Field size:
Any

Training Target
- Goalkeepers

Training Emphasis
- Crossing/owning the box
- Reactions
- Leaping power
- Positional play

Training Aspects

Skills involved:	Leaping strength, Speed of movement with ball, Quick anticipation, Outside of the foot, Trapping into space, Speed of movement off the ball, Dribbling, Quick decisions, Wing play without opponents, Quick processing, Inside of the foot, Inside of the foot passing, Inside of the laces passing, Combining technical skill with movement, Heading while in motion, Quickness of reaction, Building an attack over the wings, Volley, Laces, Quick understanding of danger
Age level:	9-12 years, 13-14 years, 15 years to Adult
Level of play:	Advanced
Type of training:	Individual training, Small group training (2-6 players)
Training structure:	Main point/Emphasis
Purpose:	Goalkeeper behaviors, Improve individual skills
Total number of players:	3 players, 4 or more players
Participating players:	Winger, Goalie
Training location:	Asphalt, Turf field, Grass field
Spatial awareness:	Limited playing field
Duration:	15-30 min
Physical skills:	Soccer-specific endurance, Strength, Power & Speed
Goalkeeper:	1 goalie, 2-5 goalies

Organization:
The goalkeeper is in the goal. One or more players (winger) stand with the balls to the side, but in line with, the penalty area. One or more players (striker) stand in the middle, but in line with the penalty area (see diagram). If no field players are available then the goalkeeper and/or the coach takes over the position.

Implementation:
The winger brings a flank player from the left into the penalty area, which is used by the striker. The goalkeeper has the opportunity to intercept the cross or save the approaching balls. He should always alternate the cross between left and right.

Passing option 1: Goalkeeper moves from his home position and intercepts the ball.
Passing option 2: Goalkeeper doesn't move to the wing and dives for the striker's first shot in the corner.

Equipment:
1 goal

Notes:

Basic steps for crosses from the side:

- The goalkeeper positions himself in the middle of the goal (1-2 steps in front of the goal line), looking in the direction of the passing player. Due to his side positioning, it is possible for him to run forward quickly in the direction of the first post. Likewise, he's in a good position to run to the goal box or the far post.
- For each cross, the goalkeeper must estimate whether he can intercept or must wait on the line.
- If the goalkeeper decides to intercept the cross, he must start with tackling the striker. In other words, he has to forcefully and consistently get to the ball to intercept at the highest possible point.

- If he decides to wait on the line, and this is clear to the striker, then he must hold onto the ball. If he's unable to do this, the ball should be parried to the side.
- Just before ball contact from the shot, the goalkeeper jumps forward or takes a step forward, spreads his arms out to the side, bends his knees a bit and stands on the balls of his feet. His feet should point in the direction of the shooter and are about shoulder-width apart. His upper body should be bent forward slightly and his eyes fixed on the ball.

Field size:

50 x 25 m

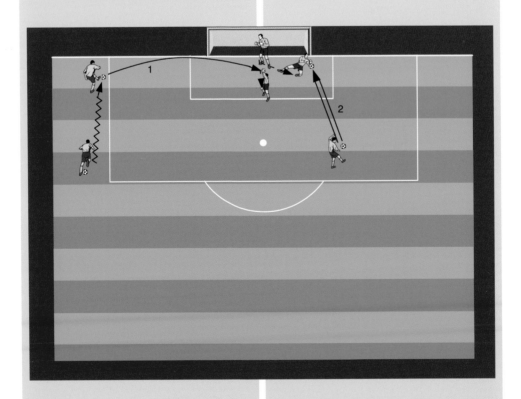

Training Target
- Goalkeepers

Training Emphasis
- Explosiveness
- Reactions
- Leaping power

Training Aspects

Skills involved:	Leaping strength, Quick anticipation, Speed of movement off the ball, Quick decisions, Quick processing, Quickness of reaction, Quick understanding of danger
Age level:	Any age
Level of play:	Recreational
Type of training:	Individual training, Small group training (2-6 players)
Training structure:	Progression, Main point/Emphasis
Purpose:	Improve individual skills
Total number of players:	2 or more players, Single player
Participating players:	Goalie
Training location:	Any
Spatial awareness:	Penalty box
Duration:	5-15 min
Physical skills:	Strength endurance, Power & Speed

Organization:
The goalkeeper stands about 12m in front of the goal and 5m from the goalkeeper coach. The goalkeeper coach has the balls.

Implementation:
The goalkeeper stands with his legs apart in front of the goalkeeper coach, who plays the ball through the goalkeeper's legs. The goalkeeper must now quickly pivot and hold the ball while jumping. If he is able to do this, he should leave the ball and immediately face the goalkeeper coach. If he's unable to do this, he should try to get the ball before it crosses the goal line.

Equipment:
1 goal

Notes:
- The goalkeeper stands softly on the balls of his feet. He should position himself as he would just before a shot.
- As soon as the ball goes through his legs, he must pivot as quickly as possible and push forcefully off from the ground and try to get the ball by making a dive.
- Quick sequence of reaction: turn push off, jump, ball control, standing up and getting into a new position.

Field size:
16 x 16 m

Training Target
- Goalkeepers

Training Emphasis
- Throws
- Finesse on the ball
- Passing

Training Aspects

Skills involved:	Speed of movement with ball, Quick anticipation, Controlling the ball, Speed of movement off the ball, Quick decisions, Quick processing, Inside of the foot, Inside of the foot passing, Inside of the laces passing, Combining technical skill with movement, Short passing, Laces
Age level:	Any age
Level of play:	Recreational
Type of training:	Small group training (2-6 players)
Training structure:	Warm-up, Progression
Purpose:	Improve individual skills
Total number of players:	2 or more players
Participating players:	Goalie
Training location:	Any
Spatial awareness:	Free space
Duration:	10 min
Physical skills:	Soccer-specific endurance

Organization:
Two goalkeepers stand opposite each other. Each goalkeeper has a ball. The distance between them varies between 10 and 30 meters, depending on the strength of the shot or throw and the age of the group.

Implementation:
Both goalkeepers adapt to the movement of the balls. The pass sequence (control/delivery) is done by both goalkeepers at the same time. Later, one ball will be thrown and the other passed.

Combination of movements/pass and throw sequences:
A – 1=flat pass, 2=control, 3=flat return pass
B – 1=waist-high ball, 2=catch the ball, 3=throw the ball back
C – 1=flat ball, 2=receive ball, 3=roll the ball back

Notes:
- A neat and pressured pass is necessary.
- Use different procedures, e.g., pass to the right, control to the side with left contact, pass to the right, etc.
- The goalkeeper must always make sure that his procedures are carried out together (simultaneous passes/throws/rolls).

Field size:
Any

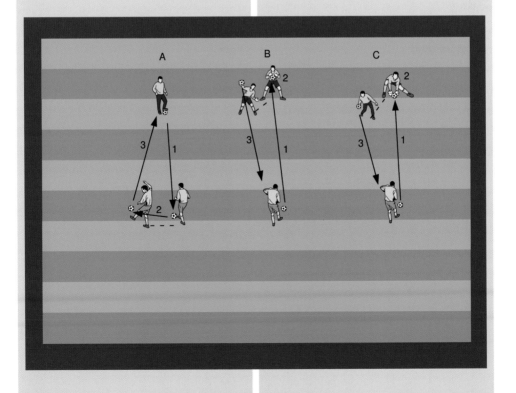

Training Target
- Goalkeepers

Training Emphasis
- Explosiveness
- Reactions
- Leaping power

Training Aspects

Skills involved:	Leaping strength, Quick anticipation, Flexibility, Speed of movement off the ball Quick decisions, Quick processing, Quickness of reaction, Quick understanding of danger
Age level:	Any age
Level of play:	Recreational
Type of training:	Individual training, Small group training (2-6 players)
Training structure:	Main point/Emphasis
Purpose:	Goalkeeper behaviors, Improve individual skills
Total number of players:	2 or more players
Participating players:	Goalie
Training location:	Any
Spatial awareness:	Penalty box
Duration:	15-25 min
Physical skills:	Power & Speed

Organization:
The goalkeeper stands in the goal, one goalkeeper coach stands between 10 and 16 m away and the other stands behind the goal. The coach behind the goal has one soccer ball and the coach in front of the goal has the rest of the balls.

Implementation:
The goalkeeper stands with his back to the goalkeeper coach. On the coach's command, the goalkeeper pivots towards the goalkeeper coach and tries to save the shot.

Equipment:
1 goal

Notes:
- The goalkeeper reacts to a previously agreed signal (nearer the game a visual signal is used). For example, the trainer passes the ball into the goal. The signal could also be a shout, raising an arm or the coach/player behind the goal dropping the ball.
- As soon as the goalkeeper has pivoted around, the coach takes the shot.
- The goalkeeper tries to save the shots. If he's unable to do this, the balls should be parried to the side.
- The take-off takes place with either no intermediate steps or just one. Several steps are a waste of time. The bodyweight determines the take-off height with the push-off leg.

The goalkeeper jumps with force to the side. He slows his momentum over his right foot and pushes off the ground with the balls of his feet. To the left, he slows his momentum over his left foot.

Field size:
16 x 16 m

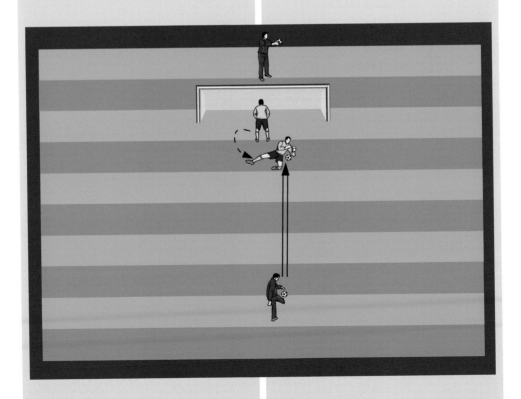

Training Target
- Goalkeepers

Training Emphasis
- Explosiveness
- Reactions
- Leaping power
- Positional play
- Shooting

Training Aspects

Skills involved:	Leaping strength, Speed of movement with ball, Quick anticipation, Outside of the foot, Speed of movement off the ball, Quick decisions, Quick processing, Inside of the foot, Inside of the foot passing, Inside of the laces passing, Combining technical skill with movement, Quickness of reaction, Laces, Quick understanding of danger
Age level:	Any age
Level of play:	Recreational
Type of training:	Group training
Training structure:	Conclusion, Main point/Emphasis
Purpose:	Training for fun, Goalkeeper behaviors, Improve individual skills
Total number of players:	12 players, 13 or more players
Participating players:	Whole team
Training location:	Any
Spatial awareness:	Penalty box
Duration:	10-30 min
Physical skills:	Soccer-specific endurance, Power & Speed
Goalkeeper:	3 goalies

Organization:
Set up three adjacent goals. A goalkeeper stands in each goal. The player stands 14-20 meters in front of the goal, each with a ball, in three rows.

Implementation:
Every third player shoots at the same time. Each player shoots at a goal. The goalkeepers have to stop goals being scored in their goal.

Options:
a) Goalkeeper competition (whoever saves the fewest goals loses) or goalkeepers vs. strikers
b) After each pass, the goalkeepers must change the goal (or move counter-clockwise). The coach gives the striker the signal to shoot.

Equipment:
1 large goal, 2 small goals

Notes:
- Just before the striker touches the ball, the goalkeeper does a small jump with both legs or takes a small step forward, spreads his arms out to the side, bends his knees slightly and stands on the balls of his feet.
- His feet should point in the direction of the striker and are about hip-width apart. The upper body is bent slightly forward and his eyes remain fixed on the ball.
- His body must always be behind the ball in the defense position.
- In the defense position, the goalkeeper must never fall backwards, but only forward.

- The goalkeeper jumps with force to the side or forward. He slows momentum over his right foot and pushes off the ground with the balls of his feet. To the left, he slows his momentum over his left foot.
- The goalkeeper tries to save the balls. If he is unable to do this, the balls should be parried to the side.
- Alternative option: As soon as the goalkeeper makes a save, he must run to the next goal because he doesn't know when the striker will take the next shot.

Field size:
30 x 25 m

Training Target
- Goalkeepers

Training Emphasis
- **Explosiveness**
- **Reactions**
- **Leaping power**
- **Positional play**
- **Shooting**

Training Aspects	
Skills involved:	Speed of movement with ball, Quick anticipation, Outside of the foot, Flexibility, Speed of movement off the ball, Quick decisions, Quick processing, Inside of the foot, Inside of the laces passing, Combining technical skill with movement, Quickness of reaction, Laces, Quick understanding of danger
Age level:	Any age
Type of training:	Group training
Training structure:	Conclusion, Main point/Emphasis
Purpose:	Improve individual skills
Total number of players:	2 or more players
Participating players:	Whole team
Training location:	Any
Spatial awareness:	Penalty box
Duration:	10-15 min
Physical skills:	Strength endurance, Power & Speed
Goalkeeper:	1 goalie, 2 goalies

Organization:
The goalkeeper is in the goal. One or more players stand roughly 20 m in front of the goal. The players have the soccer balls.

Implementation:
The players take turns shooting at the goal. Three consecutive goals scored means 10 push-ups for the goalkeeper, 3 saved goals mean 10 push-ups for the players.

Equipment:
1 goal

Notes:
- Just before the player touches the ball, the goalkeeper does a small jump with both legs or takes a small step forward, spreads his arms out to the side, bends his knees slightly and stands on the balls of his feet. His feet should point in the direction of the player and are about hip-width apart, the upper body is bent slightly forward and his eyes remain fixed on the ball.
- His body must always be behind the ball in the defense position.
- In the defense position, the goalkeeper must never fall backwards, only forward.
- The goalkeeper jumps with force to the side or forward. He slows his momentum over his right foot and pushes off the ground with the balls of his feet. To the left, he slows his momentum over his left foot.

- The goalkeeper tries to save the balls. If he is unable to do this, the balls should be parried to the side.
- The distance between the shooters may vary between 8 and 20 meters, depending on the age of the group.

Field size:
25 x 25 m

Training Target
- Goalkeepers

Training Emphasis
- Explosiveness
- Reactions
- Coordination

Training Aspects

Skills involved:	Leaping strength, Quick anticipation, Speed of movement off the ball, Quick decisions, Quick processing, Quickness of reaction, Quick understanding of danger
Age level:	Any age
Level of play:	Advanced
Type of training:	Individual training, Small group training (2-6 players)
Training structure:	Warm-up, Progression
Purpose:	Improve individual skills
Total number of players:	2 or more players, Single player
Participating players:	Goalie
Training location:	Any
Spatial awareness:	Penalty box
Duration:	10-15 min
Physical skills:	Soccer-specific endurance, Power & Speed

Organization:
Set up a row of small hurdles in front of the goal. The goalkeeper is in the goal, and the goalkeeper coach stands with the balls about 10m in front of the hurdles.

Implementation:
The goalkeeper runs with his knees up or skips over the hurdles. Then he makes a volley or drop kick shot to the goalkeeper coach in the goalkeeper's catching area. Repeat this 4 or 5 times. The goalkeeper runs with his knees up or skips over the hurdles sideways, then the coach can aim his shots slightly to the left or right.

Equipment:
1 goal, 6 hurdles, 6 rings

Notes:
- Quick and neat use of techniques over the hurdles.
- Skipping => short, quick movements using the balls of the feet (not the whole foot). Heels must not touch the ground, arms/legs are bent and swing as they would naturally in a counter movement (right arm/left foot). The upper body is bent forward. Little contact is made with the ground, high speed is necessary.
- Knees up => the right leg is bent at the highest possible angle. The left (bent) arm does the same in an upward movement. The left leg is almost stretched out. The player stands on the balls of his feet. He places the ball of his right foot on the ground and does the same sequence of movements with the left. The upper body is upright. Little contact is made with the ground, high speed is necessary.

- As soon as the goalkeeper has passed the last hurdle, the coach takes a shot.
- Just before the coach touches the ball, the goalkeeper does a small jump with both legs or takes a small step forward, spreads his arms out to the side, bends his knees slightly and stands on the balls of his feet. His feet should point in the direction of the trainer and are about hip-width apart. His upper body is bent slightly forward and eyes remain fixed on the ball.
- His body must always be behind the ball in the defense position.
- In the defense position the goalkeeper must never fall backwards, only forward.
- Side-shifted jumps (ski jump/movements) => with a slightly forward-leaning upper body, alternate jumping diagonally forward with the right and left leg (with the right leg, jump forward to the right, and to the left with the left leg) Here it's important that the balls of the feet are used for take-off and landing. The arms swing supportively. Repositioning the standing leg after the take-off and the other leg should be bent (no ground contact). The player should be facing forward.

Field size:
20 x 20 m

Placement of hurdles:
Distance from goal line to first hurdle: 3 m
Distance between hurdles: 1 m

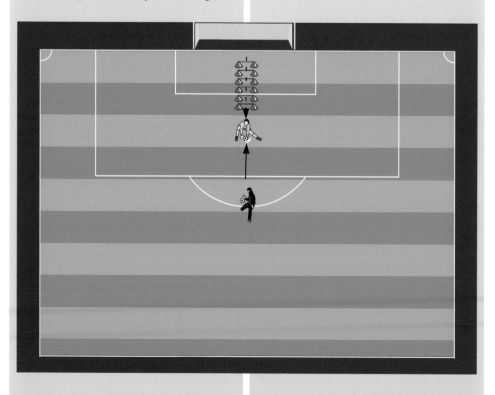

Training Target
- Goalkeepers

Training Emphasis
- Explosiveness
- Coordination
- Reactions
- Speed
- Leaping power

Training Aspects

Skills involved:	Leaping strength, Quick anticipation, Speed of movement off the ball, Quick decisions, Quick processing, Quickness of reaction, Quick understanding of danger
Age level:	Any age
Level of play:	Advanced
Type of training:	Individual training, Group training
Training structure:	Warm-up, Progression
Purpose:	Improve individual skills
Total number of players:	2 or more players, Single player
Participating players:	Goalie
Training location:	Any
Spatial awareness:	Penalty box
Duration:	10-15 min
Physical skills:	Soccer-specific endurance, Power & Speed

Organization:
Set up a hoop course like the image. The goalkeeper stands on the goal line, the goalkeeper coach stands with the balls in the penalty area.

Implementation:
The goalkeeper does a ski jump through the rings without touching them. Then the goalkeeper coach shoots a flat ball 1 or 2 meters to the left or right of the goalkeeper. The goalkeeper must catch the ball.

Alternative:
The goalkeeper jumps through the hoops with his legs together, then the coach makes a volley or a bouncing shot.

Equipment:
1 goal, 6 hoops

Notes:
- Quick and neat use of techniques over the hoops.
- Side-shifted jumps (ski jump/movements) => with a slightly forward-leaning upper body, alternate jumping diagonally forward with the right and left leg (with the right leg, jump forward to the right, and to the left with the left leg). Here it's important that the balls of the feet are used for take-off and landing. The arms swing supportively. Reposition the standing leg after the take-off and the other leg should be bent (no ground contact). The player should be facing forward.
- As soon as the goalkeeper has passed the last hoop, the coach takes a shot.
- Just before the coach touches the ball, the goalkeeper does a small jump with both legs or takes a small step forward, spreads his arms out to the side, bends his knees slightly and stands on the balls of his feet. His feet should point in the

direction of the trainer and are about hip-width apart. The upper body is bent slightly forward and eyes remain fixed on the ball.

- His body must always be behind the ball in the defense position.
- In the defense position, the goalkeeper must never fall backwards, only forward.

Field size:
16 x 16 m

Placement of hoops:
Distance from goal line to first hoop: 2 m

Training Target
- Goalkeepers

Training Emphasis
- Throw-ins
- Explosiveness
- Reactions
- Leaping power
- Positional play

Training Aspects

Skills involved:	Leaping strength, Speed of movement with ball, Quick anticipation, Speed of movement off the ball, Quick decisions, Quick processing, Inside of the foot, Combining technical skill with movement, Quickness of reaction, Laces, Quick understanding of danger
Age level:	Any age
Level of play:	Recreational
Type of training:	Individual training, Small group training (2-6 players)
Training structure:	Warm-up, Progression
Purpose:	Improve individual skills
Total number of players:	2 or more players, Single player
Participating players:	Goalie
Training location:	Any
Duration:	1-10 min
Physical skills:	Soccer-specific endurance, Power & Speed

Organization:
The goalkeeper is in the goal. The goalkeeper coach positions himself 10-16 meters in front of the goal with the balls.

Implementation:
The goalkeeper coach changes between playing volley and drop kick shots to the goalkeeper. Repeat approximately 20 times.

Equipment:
1 goal

Notes:
- Just before the coach touches the ball, the goalkeeper does a small jump with both legs or takes a small step forward, spreads his arms out to the side, bends his knees slightly and stands on the balls of his feet. His feet should point in the direction of the trainer and are about hip-width apart. The upper body is bent slightly forward and the eyes remain fixed on the ball.
- His body must always be behind the ball in the defense position.
- In the defense position, the goalkeeper must never fall backwards, only forward.
- The caught ball is thrown back to the coach.

Field size:
16 x 16 m

Training Target
- Goalkeepers

Training Emphasis
- **Explosiveness**
- **Reactions**
- **Leaping power**

Training Aspects

Skills involved:	Leaping strength, Quick anticipation, Speed of movement off the ball, Quick decisions, Quick processing, Quickness of reaction, Speed in change of direction, Sprightliness, Quick understanding of danger
Age level:	Any age
Level of play:	Recreational
Type of training:	Individual training, Small group training (2-6 players)
Training structure:	Warm-up, Progression
Purpose:	Improve individual skills
Total number of players:	2 or more players, Single player
Participating players:	Goalie
Training location:	Any
Spatial awareness:	Penalty box
Duration:	5-10 min
Physical skills:	Soccer-specific endurance, Power & Speed

Organization:
The goalkeeper is in the goal. The goalkeeper coach is 10-16 meters in front of the goal. The goalkeeper coach has the soccer balls.

Implementation:
The goalkeeper runs to the goal area and stands there. Then the coach plays a volley or drop kick shot to the goalkeeper in the catching area. The goalkeeper then goes back to the line. Repeat 6-8 times.

Equipment:
1 goal

Notes:
- Quick start or sprint to the line.
- Just before the coach touches the ball, the goalkeeper does a small jump with both legs or takes a small step forward, spreads his arms out to the side, bends his knees slightly and stands on the balls of his feet. His feet should point in the direction of the trainer and are about hip-width apart. His upper body is bent slightly forward and his eyes remain fixed on the ball.
- His body must always be behind the ball in the defense position.
- In the defense position, the goalkeeper must never fall backwards, only forward.

Field size:
16 x 16 m

Training Target
- **Goalkeepers**

Training Emphasis
- **Coordination**
- **Reactions**

Training Aspects

Skills involved:	Leaping strength, Speed of movement with ball, Quick anticipation, Control, Speed of movement off the ball, Quick decisions, Quick processing, Combining technical skill with movement, Running technique with/without ball, Quickness of reaction, Speed in change of direction, Quick understanding of danger
Age level:	Any age
Level of play:	Recreational
Type of training:	Individual training, Small group training (2-6 players)
Training structure:	Warm-up, Progression
Purpose:	Improve individual skills
Total number of players:	2 or more players, Single player
Participating players:	Goalie
Training location:	Any
Spatial awareness:	Penalty box
Duration:	5-15 min
Physical skills:	Soccer-specific endurance, Power & Speed

Organization:
The goalkeeper is in the goal. The goalkeeper coach is 10-16 meters in front of the goal. Goalkeeper coach has the soccer balls.

Implementation:
The goalkeeper sidesteps from post to post. While he's doing this, the goalkeeper coach shoots a volley in the goalkeeper's catching area. The caught ball is thrown back to the coach.
Complete 3-5 rounds, 6-8 balls per round.

Equipment:
1 goal

Notes:
- Quick sideways movements on the balls of the feet.
- If the ball is caught the thumbs touch the middle of the ball in front of the body and the fingers are spread out.
- Body tension is important here.

Training Target
- **Goalkeepers**

Training Emphasis
- **Coordination**
- **Reactions**

Training Aspects

Skills involved:	Leaping strength, Quick anticipation, Control, Speed of movement off the ball, Quick decisions, Quick processing, Quickness of reaction, Quick understanding of danger
Age level:	Any age
Level of play:	Recreational
Type of training:	Individual training, Small group training (2-6 players)
Training structure:	Warm-up, Progression
Purpose:	Improve individual skills
Total number of players:	2 or more players, Single player
Participating players:	Goalie
Training location:	Any
Duration:	5 min
Physical skills:	Soccer-specific endurance, Power & Speed

Organization:
The goalkeeper is in the goal. The goalkeeper coach positions himself with the balls 10-16 meters in front of the goal.

Implementation:
The coach plays a diagonal ball in line with the cross bar alternating from right to left. The goalkeeper runs towards the baseline and tries to catch the ball.
Play 4 balls per side.

Equipment:
1 goal

Notes:
- Run on the balls of your feet; don't use the whole of your foot or heels
- Soft, light movements; don't stomp, be light-footed.

- The goalkeeper must always move on the balls of his feet and shouldn't fall backwards. He should learn to always keep an eye on the ball until he has it under control.
- Just before the coach touches the ball, the goalkeeper does a small jump with both legs or takes a small step forward, spreads his arms out to the side, bends his knees slightly and stands on the balls of his feet. His feet should point in the direction of the coach and are about hip-width apart. The upper body is bent slightly forward and the eyes remain fixed on the ball.
- His body must always be behind the ball in the defense position.
- In the defense position, the goalkeeper must never fall backwards, only forward.
- The caught ball is thrown back to the coach.

Field size:
16 x 16 m

Training Target
- Goalkeepers

Training Emphasis
- **Explosiveness**
- **Coordiantion**
- **Reactions**
- **Speed**
- **Leaping power**

Training Aspects

Skills involved:	Leaping strength, Speed of movement with ball, Quick anticipation, Control, Speed of movement off the ball, Half-volley, Quick processing, Combining technical skill with movement, Quickness of reaction, Quick understanding of danger
Age level:	Any age
Level of play:	Recreational
Type of training:	Individual training, Small group training (2-6 players)
Training structure:	Warm-up, Progression
Purpose:	Improve individual skills
Total number of players:	2 or more players, Single player
Participating players:	Goalie
Training location:	Any
Spatial awareness:	Free space
Duration:	5-20 min
Physical skills:	Soccer-specific endurance, Strength endurance, Power & Speed
Goalkeeper:	1 goalie

Organization:
Set up a hoop course as shown in the diagram. The goalkeeper stands behinds the first ring. The goalkeeper coach stands 16-20 meters away with the balls.

Implementation:
The goalkeeper jumps as fast as he can through the hoops without touching them. He then receives a powerful drop kick shot from the coach in the catching area.

Alternative:
The goalkeeper skips or runs with his knees up through the hoops, then the goalkeeper coach does a volley shot or a bounce pass.

Equipment:
1 goal, 5 hoops

Notes:
- It's important that the players don't touch the hoops.
- Palms remain open, don't make a fist.
- Run on the balls of your feet, don't use your whole foot or heels.
- Make little contact with the ground.
- Knees up => the right leg is bent at the highest possible angle. The left (bent) arm does the same in an upward movement. The left leg is almost stretched out. The player stands on the balls of his feet. He places the ball of his right foot on the ground and does the same sequence of movements with the left. The upper body is upright. Make little contact with the ground, high speed is necessary.
- Skipping using the whole foot=> small leg movement. Roll back and forth on your

foot from your toes to your heel. Bend your arms and lean forward slightly.

- Just before the coach touches the ball, the goalkeeper does a small jump with both legs or takes a small step forward, spreads his arms out to the side, bends his knees slightly and stands on the balls of his feet. His feet should point in the direction of the coach and are about hip-width apart. The upper body is bent slightly forward and the eyes remain fixed on the ball.
- His body must always be behind the ball in the defense position.
- In the defense position, the goalkeeper must never fall backwards, only forward.

Field size:
10 x 20 m

Distance between rings:
The distance between the rings depends on the age of the players. It's best to try it once with the kids before you set a distance.

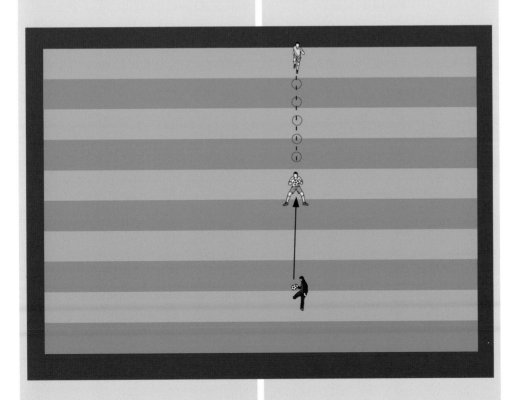

137

Training Target
- Goalkeepers

Training Emphasis
- **Coordiantion**
- **Reactions**

Training Aspects

Skills involved:	Leaping strength, Quick anticipation, Control, Flexibility, Speed of movement off the ball, Quick decisions, Quick processing, Quickness of reaction, Speed in change of direction, Quick understanding of danger
Age level:	Any age
Level of play:	Recreational
Type of training:	Individual training, Small group training (2-6 players)
Training structure:	Warm-up, Progression
Purpose:	Improve individual skills
Total number of players:	2 or more players, Single player
Participating players:	Goalie
Training location:	Any
Spatial awareness:	Penalty box
Duration:	10-15 min
Physical skills:	Soccer-specific endurance, Power & Speed

Organization:
Set up a cone course as shown in the diagram. The goalkeeper stands on the goal line, the goalkeeper coach stands on the penalty line with the balls.

Implementation:
The goalkeeper sidesteps between the cones, squats and touches the cone on his left with his left hand, or the cone on the right with his right hand.
The coach then shoots a flat shot to the side of him from either the right or left.

Intensity:
5-6 repetitions

Alternative:
- The goalkeeper sidesteps backwards between the cones and touches the cones with his right or left hand, depending on the placement of the cones. When he's

done this, he turns around and receives a volley or bounce shot from the coach.

Equipment:
1 goal, 6 cones

Notes:
- Forward/backwards sidesteps=› when running sideways, the legs are parallel, alternating between being together and apart. Arms swing in sync with the leg movements.
- Just before the coach touches the ball the goalkeeper does a small jump with both legs or takes a small step forward, spreads his arms out to the side, bends his knees slightly and stands on the balls of his feet. His feet should point in the direction of the coach and are about hip-width apart. His upper body is bent slightly forward and his eyes remain fixed on the ball.

- His body must always be behind the ball in the defense position.
- In the defense position, the goalkeeper must never fall backwards, only forward.
- Side-shifted jumps (ski jump/movements) => with a slightly forward-leaning upper body, alternate jumping diagonally forward with the right and left leg (with the right leg, jump forward to the right and to the left with the left leg) Here it's important that the balls of the feet are used for take-off and landing. The arms swing supportively. Reposition the standing leg after the take-off and the other leg should be bent (no ground contact). The player should be facing forward.

Field size:
16 x 16 m

Distance between cones:
Goal line to first cone: 3 m
Length: 2 m
Width: 3 m

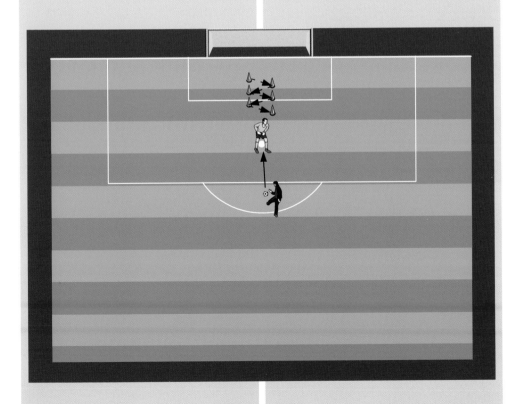

Training Target
- Goalkeepers

Training Emphasis
- **Coordiantion**
- **Reactions**
- **Leaping power**

Training Aspects

Skills involved:	Leaping strength, Quick anticipation, Control, Speed of movement off the ball, Quick decisions, Quick processing, Quickness of reaction, Quick understanding of danger
Age level:	Any age
Level of play:	Recreational
Type of training:	Individual training, Small group training (2-6 players)
Training structure:	Warm-up, Progression
Purpose:	Improve individual skills
Total number of players:	2 or more players, Single player
Participating players:	Goalie
Training location:	Any
Spatial awareness:	Penalty box
Duration:	10-15 min
Physical skills:	Soccer-specific endurance, Power & Speed

Organization:
Set up an obstacle course with rods like the diagram. The goalkeeper stands to the side of the construction, the goalkeeper coach stands 15 meters away on the other side with the balls.

Implementation:
The goalkeeper side steps through the rods. It's important here that this exercise is done precisely, so that none of the rods are touched. Small steps should be taken at high speed. When the goalkeeper reaches the end of the course, the goalkeeper coach takes a flat shot in the direction of the goal.

Intensity:
5-7 repetitions

Equipment:
1 goal, 5 hurdles, 5 rods

Notes:
- Forward/backwards sidesteps=› when running sideways, the legs are parallel, alternating between being together and apart. Arms swing in sync with the leg movements.
- As soon as the goalkeeper has passed the last hurdle, the coach makes the shot.
- Just before the coach touches the ball, the goalkeeper makes a small jump with both legs or takes a small step forward, spreads his arms out to the side, bends his knees slightly and stands on the balls of his feet. His feet should point in the direction of the coach and are about hip-width apart. The upper body is bent slightly forward and the eyes remain fixed on the ball.
- His body must always be behind the ball in the defense position.
- In the defense position, the goalkeeper must never fall backwards, only forward.

- Side-shifted jumps (ski jump/movements) => with a slightly forward-leaning upper body, alternate jumping diagonally forward with the right and left leg (with the right leg, jump forward to the right, and to the left with the left leg) Here it's important that the balls of the feet are used for take-off and landing. The arms swing supportively. Reposition the standing leg after the take-off and the other leg should be bent (no ground contact). The player should be facing forward.

Field size:
20 x 20 m

Placement of hurdles:
Distance between goalkeeper and the first hurdle: 3 m
Distance between hurdles: 1 m

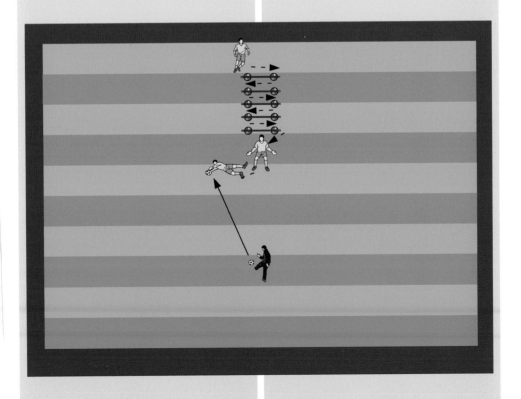

Training Target
- Goalkeepers

Training Emphasis
- Coordiantion
- Reactions

Training Aspects

Skills involved:	Leaping strength, Quick anticipation, Control, Quick decisions, Quick processing, Quickness of reaction, Quick understanding of danger
Age level:	Any age
Level of play:	Recreational
Type of training:	Individual training, Small group training (2-6 players)
Training structure:	Warm-up, Progression
Purpose:	Improve individual skills
Total number of players:	2 or more players, Single player
Participating players:	Goalie
Training location:	Any
Spatial awareness:	Free space
Duration:	10-15 min
Physical skills:	Soccer-specific endurance, Power & Speed

Organization:
Set up an obstacle course with poles as shown in the diagram. The goalkeeper stands to the side of the construction, the goalkeeper coach stands 15 meters away on the other side with the balls.

Implementation:
The goalkeeper runs with his knees high over the poles. It's important here that this exercise is done precisely, so that none of the rods are touched. Take small steps at high speed. When the goalkeeper reaches the end of the course, the goalkeeper coach makes a flat shot in the direction of the goal.

Intensity:
5-7 repetitions

Equipment:
1 goal, 5 hurdles, 5 poles

Notes:
- Knees up => the right leg is bent at the highest possible angle. The left (bent) arm does the same in an upward movement. The left leg is almost stretched out. The player stands on the balls of his feet. He places the ball of his right foot on the ground and does the same sequence of movements with the left. The upper body is upright. There is little ground contact; high speed is necessary.
- Just before the coach touches the ball, the goalkeeper makes a small jump with both legs or takes a small step forward, spreads his arms out to the side, bends his knees slightly and stands on the balls of his feet. His feet should point in the direction of the coach and are about hip-width apart. The upper body is bent slightly forward and the eyes remain fixed on the ball.
- His body must always be behind the ball in the defense position.

- In the defense position, the goalkeeper must never fall backwards, only forward.
- Side-shifted jumps (ski jump/movements) => with a slightly forward-leaning upper body, alternate jumping diagonally forward with the right and left leg (with the right leg, jump forward to the right, and to the left with the left leg) Here it's important that the balls of the feet are used for take-off and landing. The arms swing supportively. Reposition the standing leg after the take-off and the other leg should be bent (no ground contact). The player should be facing forward.

Field size:
20 x 20 m

Placement of hurdles:
Distance from goalkeeper to first hurdle: 3 m
Distance between hurdles: 1 m

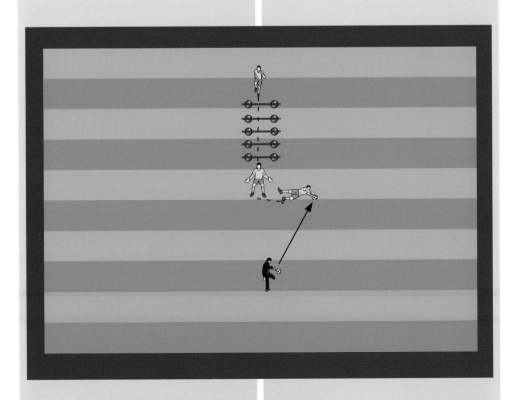

Training Target
- Goalkeepers

Training Emphasis
- Coordiantion
- Reactions

Training Aspects

Skills involved:	Leaping strength, Quick anticipation, Flexibility, Speed of movement off the ball, Quick decisions, Quick processing, Quickness of reaction, Speed in change of direction, Quick understanding of danger
Age level:	Any age
Level of play:	Recreational
Type of training:	Individual training, Small group training (2-6 players)
Training structure:	Warm-up, Progression
Purpose:	Improve individual skills
Total number of players:	2 or more players, Single player
Participating players:	Goalie
Training location:	Any
Spatial awareness:	Penalty box
Duration:	10-15 min
Physical skills:	Soccer-specific endurance, Power & Speed

Organization:
Set up an obstacle course with poles as shown in the diagram. The goalkeeper stands to the side of the construction, the goalkeeper coach stands in the penalty area with the balls.

Implementation:
The goalkeeper skips sideways over the poles. It's important here that this exercise is done precisely, so that none of the rods are touched. Make small steps, with a narrow stance at high speed. When the goalkeeper reaches the end of the course, the goalkeeper coach makes a flat shot into the corner.

Intensity:
6-8 repetitions

Equipment:
1 goal, 5 hurdles, 5 poles

Notes:
- Just before the coach touches the ball the goalkeeper makes a small jump with both legs or takes a small step forward, spreads his arms out to the side, bends his knees slightly and stands on the balls of his feet. His feet should point in the direction of the coach and are about hip-width apart. The upper body is bent slightly forward and the eyes remain fixed on the ball.
- His body must always be behind the ball in the defense position.
- Skipping => short, quick movements on the balls of your feet (don't use your whole foot). Heels must not touch the ground, legs/arms are bent and swing in time with the natural counter-movements (right arm, left leg). The upper body is bent forward. Make little contact time with the ground, high speed is necassary.

- In the defense position, the goalkeeper must never fall backwards, only forward.
- Side-shifted jumps (ski jump/movements) => with a slightly forward-leaning upper body, alternate jumping diagonally forward with the right and left leg (with the right leg, jump forward to the right, and to the left with the left leg) Here it's important that the balls of the feet are used for take-off and landing. The arms swing supportively. Reposition the standing leg after the take-off and the other leg should be bent (no ground contact). The player should be facing forward.

Field size:
16 x 16 m

Placement of hurdles:
The first hurdle is in line with the goal post
Distance to baseline: 3 m
Distance between hurdles: 1 m

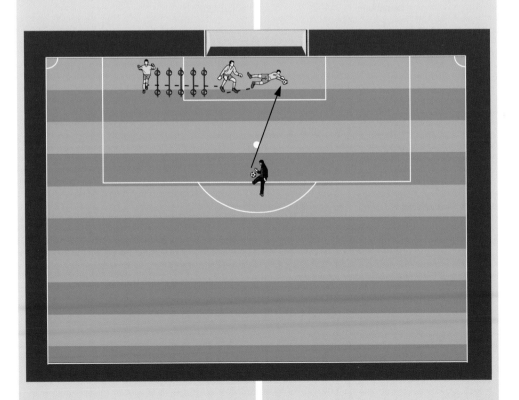

Training Target
- Goalkeepers

Training Emphasis
- **Explosiveness**
- **Reactions**
- **Leaping power**

Training Aspects

Skills involved:	Leaping strength, Quick anticipation, Control, Flexibility, Speed of movement off the ball, Quick decisions, Quick processing, Inside of the foot, Inside of the foot passing, Short passing, Quickness of reaction, Volley, Laces, Quick understanding of danger
Age level:	Any age
Level of play:	Advanced
Type of training:	Individual training, Small group training (2-6 players)
Training structure:	Main point/Emphasis
Purpose:	Improve individual skills
Total number of players:	2 or more players, Single player
Participating players:	Goalie
Training location:	Any
Spatial awareness:	Free space
Duration:	10-15 min
Physical skills:	Soccer-specific endurance, Power & Speed

Organization:
Five hurdles of varying heights of 70-100 cm (with children use lower heights according to their jumping ability) are placed behind one another. The hurdles stand 1-1.5 meters apart. The goalkeeper stands on one side of this construction, the goalkeeper coach between 12 and 16 meters away with the balls.

Implementation:
The goalkeeper performs a tuck jump (legs bent) over the hurdles. It is important to actively use the arms to support the jump

Intensity:
4 repetitions and afterwards a break of approx. 3 minutes. 5 rounds in total.

Alternatives:
After each jump, the goalkeeper has to catch a ball or pass a ball back.

Equipment:
5 hurdles

Notes:
- Tuck jump => through a powerful, two-legged take-off, the knees/thighs are pulled up to the chest. The arms are bent and swing back. The torso is up right. Land on the balls of the feet. The next jump immediately follows after a short time on the ground.
- Directly after the final tuck jump, the player has to position himself so that his standing leg is laterally offset to the ball, and the leg with which he wants to kick the ball is swung back.
- Just before the coach touches the ball the goalkeeper makes a small jump with both legs or takes a small step forward, spreads his arms out to the side, bends his knees slightly and stands on the balls of his feet. His feet should point in the

direction of the coach and are about hip-width apart. The upper body is bent slightly forward and the eyes remain fixed on the ball.
* For every defensive action, the body has to be brought behind the ball.

Field size:
20 x 20 m

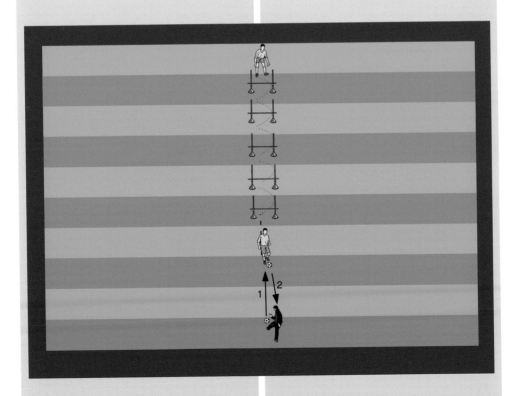

Training Target
- Goalkeepers

Training Emphasis
- **Explosiveness**
- **Coordination**
- **Reactions**
- **Leaping power**

Training Aspects

Skills involved:	Leaping strength, Quick anticipation, Control, Quick decisions, Quick processing, Inside of the foot, Combining technical skill with movement, Quickness of reaction, Volley, Laces, Quick understanding of danger
Age level:	Any age
Level of play:	Recreational
Type of training:	Individual training, Small group training (2-6 players)
Training structure:	Progression, Main point/Emphasis
Purpose:	Improve individual skills
Total number of players:	2 or more players, Single player
Participating players:	Goalie
Training location:	Any
Spatial awareness:	Free space
Duration:	10-15 min
Physical skills:	Soccer-specific endurance, Strength endurance, Power & Speed

Organization:
Six hurdles with a height of approximately 30 cm are placed 80-100cm behind each other. The goalkeeper stands on one side of the construction, the goalkeeper coach stands with the balls 12-16 meters away on the other side.

Implementation:
The goalkeeper jumps over 3 of the hurdles with his right leg and 3 with his left. Afterwards he has a recovery period of approximately 2 minutes. 4 rounds in total.

Alternatives:
After the jumps, the goalkeeper has to catch or pass a ball.

Equipment:
6 hurdles

Notes:
- Run on the balls of the feet, not on the whole foot/heel.
- Tread loosely and lightly, don't stomp.
- The arms bent towards the body alternate in conjunction with the legs, not away from the body.
- Short ground-time.
- One-legged jumps=› develops the ability to push off. Increasing explosive power with restricted goal-kicking time improves take-off speed. Jump forward and land on the ball of the right foot. Make short contact with the ground with an explosive sprint. The left foot hits the ground in the front.
- Just before the coach makes contact with the ball, the goalkeeper performs a short, forward two-legged preparatory jump, or takes a short step forward. Spreads his arms, bends his legs slightly and stands on the balls of his feet. The feet point in the direction of the coach and are hip-distance

apart. The torso is bent slightly forward and the eyes are fixed on the ball.
- For every defensive action, the body has to be brought behind the ball.
- During defensive actions, the goalkeeper must never fall backwards but rather forward.

Field size:
20 x 20 m

Placement of hurdles:
Distance between goalkeepers to the first hurdle: 3 m

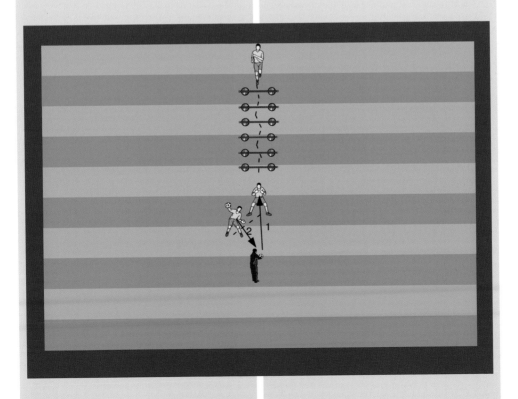

Training Target
- Goalkeepers

Training Emphasis
- Reactions
- Leaping power

Training Aspects

Skills involved:	Leaping strength, Quick anticipation, Control, Flexibility, Speed of movement off the ball, Quick decisions, Quickness of reaction, Quick understanding of danger
Age level:	Any age
Level of play:	Recreational
Type of training:	Individual training, Small group training (2-6 players)
Training structure:	Main point/Emphasis
Purpose:	Improve individual skills
Total number of players:	2 or more players, Single player
Participating players:	Goalie
Training location:	Any
Spatial awareness:	Penalty box
Duration:	10-25 min
Physical skills:	Strength endurance, Power & Speed

Organization:

The goalkeeper stands on the goal line, the goalkeeper coach stands with the balls on the penalty line.

Implementation:

The goalkeeper stands on the goal line with his back to the coach and performs 3-5 tuck jumps, each time touching the crossbar. After the final jump, he spins to face the coach and reacts to his shot.

Intensity:

4-6 repetitions

Equipment:

1 Full-size goal.

Notes:

- Tuck jump => through a powerful, two-legged take off, the knees/thighs are pulled up to the chest. The arms are bent and swing back. The torso is upright.

Land on the balls of the feet. The next jump immediately follows after a short ground-time.

- Fast 90-degree spin toward the coach.
- If possible, just before the coach makes contact with the ball, the goalkeeper performs a short, forward two-legged preparatory jump, or takes a short step forwards. Spreads his arms, bends his legs slightly and stands on the balls of his feet. The feet point in the direction of the coach and are at hip-distance apart. The torso is bent slightly forward and the eyes are fixed on the ball.
- For every defensive action, the body has to be brought behind the ball.
- During defensive actions, the goalkeeper must never fall backwards but rather forward.
- Laterally shifted jumps (skier jump/movement) => with a torso bent slightly forward, jump forward with alternating right and left legs (with the

right leg, forward right and with the left, forward left). It is important that the take-off and landing occur on the balls of the feet, whereby the arms swing supportively. When the standing leg lands after the jump, the other leg is bent (no ground-time). Look straight ahead.

Field size:
Penalty area

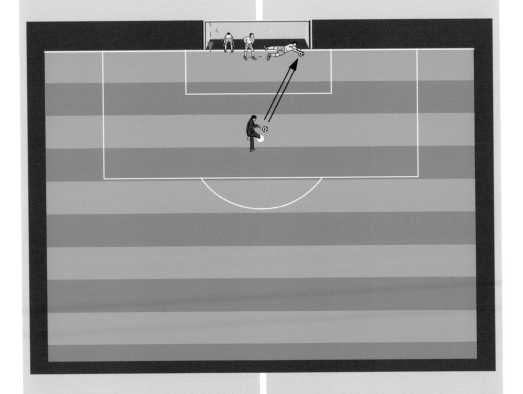

Training Target
- Activation/Warm-up

Training Emphasis
- Explosiveness
- Reactions
- Leaping power

Training Aspects

Skills involved:	Leaping strength, Quick anticipation, Control, Flexibility, Speed of movement off the ball, Quick decisions, Quick processing, Quickness of reaction, Speed in change of direction, Quick understanding of danger
Age level:	Any age
Level of play:	Recreational
Type of training:	Individual training, Small group training (2-6 players)
Training structure:	Main point/Emphasis
Purpose:	Improve individual skills
Total number of players:	2 or more players, Single player
Participating players:	Goalie
Training location:	Any
Spatial awareness:	Penalty box
Duration:	10-15 min
Physical skills:	Strength, Power & Speed

Organization:
A hurdle is constructed 3-4 meters in front of the goal line. The goalkeeper stands in centre of the goal on the goal line and the goalkeeper coach takes up a position 12 meters away as shown in the diagram.

Implementation:
On the command of the coach, the goalkeeper jumps over the approx. 1m high hurdle. The start signal is either the GC's body movement or the dropping of the ball. After jumping over the hurdle a mid-height throw in the right or left corner follows.

Intensity:
6 repetitions in each corner.

Equipment:
1 full-size goal, 1 hurdle

Notes:
- Squat jumps => through a powerful, two-legged take-off, the knees/thighs are pulled up to the chest. The arms are bent and swing back. The torso is upright. Land on the balls of the feet. The next jump immediately follows after short ground-time.
- Landing occurs on the balls of the feet. The feet point in the direction of the coach and are approximately hip distance. The torso is bent slightly forward and the eyes are fixed on the ball. The landing and take-off occur fluidly into each other and are a single movement.
- For every defensive action, the body has to be brought behind the ball.
- During defensive actions, the goalkeeper must never fall backwards but rather forward.
- Laterally shifted jumps (skier jump/movement) => with a torso bent

slightly forward, jump forward while alternating right and left legs (with the right leg move towards the right and with the left move forward left). It is important that the take-off and landing occur on the balls of the feet, whereby the arms swing supportively. When the standing leg lands after the jump, the other leg is bent (no ground-time). Look straight ahead.

Field size:
Penalty area

Placement of hurdles:
Distance between the goal line and hurdle: 3 m
Coach stands on the penalty line.

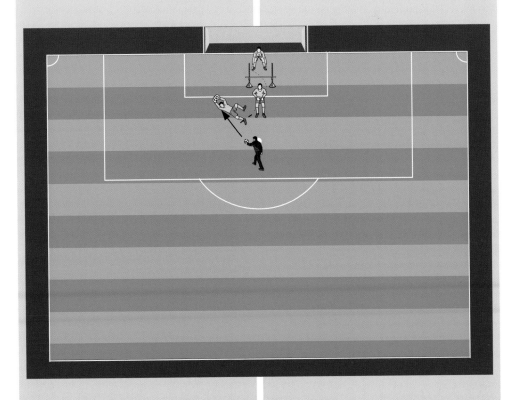

Training Target
- Goalkeepers

Training Emphasis
- **Explosiveness**
- **Reactions**
- **Leaping power**

Training Aspects

Skills involved:	Leaping strength, Quick anticipation, Control, Speed of movement off the ball, Quick decisions, Quick processing, Quickness of reaction, Quick understanding of danger
Age level:	Any age
Level of play:	Recreational
Type of training:	Individual training, Small group training (2-6 players)
Training structure:	Main point/Emphasis
Purpose:	Improve individual skills
Total number of players:	2 or more players, Single player
Participating players:	Goalie
Training location:	Any
Spatial awareness:	Penalty box
Duration:	10-20 min
Physical skills:	Strength endurance, Power & Speed

Organization:
Construct an obstacle course, as shown in the diagram. The goalkeeper stands on one side of the course, the goalkeeper coach stands with the balls on the penalty line.

Implementation:
The goalkeeper laterally jumps with one leg over the stanchions. After the last stanchion, the coach throws a high ball at the goal, so that the goalkeeper really has to stretch in order to reach the ball.

Intensity:
4-6 balls. Afterwards change legs.

Equipment:
1 full-size goal, 5 stanchions

Notes:
- One-legged jumps=> serve the development of the ability to push off. (increasing maximum and explosive power with restricted goal kicking time), that is to say the take-off speed. Jump forwards off and land on the right foot's ball of the foot. Short contact with the floor with an explosive sprint. The left foot hits the ground to the front.
- Short ground-time.
- For every defensive action, the body has to be brought behind the ball.
- Laterally shifted jumps (skier jump/movement) => with a torso bent slightly forward, jump off forward with alternating right and left legs (with the right leg, jump forward right and with the left jump forward left). It is important that the take off and landing occur on the balls of the feet, whereby the arms swing supportively. When the standing leg lands after the jump, the other leg is bent (no ground-time). Look straight ahead.

Field size:
Penalty area

Placement of hurdles:
The first hurdle is in line with the post.
Distance to byline: 3 m
Distance between hurdles: 1 m

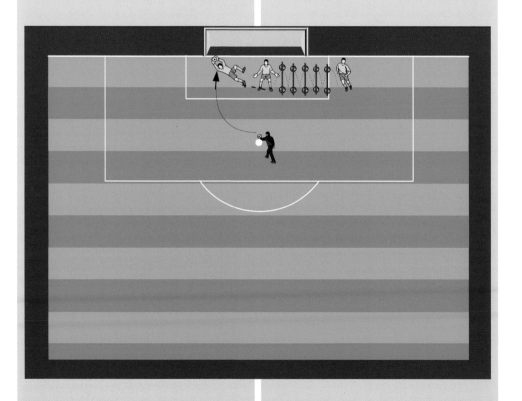

Training Target
- Goalkeepers

Training Emphasis
- Explosiveness
- Reactions

Training Aspects

Skills involved:	Leaping strength, Speed of movement with ball, Quick anticipation, Trapping, Control, Speed of movement off the ball, Quick decisions, Quick processing, Quickness of reaction, Speed in change of direction, Quick understanding of danger
Age level:	Any age
Level of play:	Recreational
Type of training:	Group training
Training structure:	Main point/Emphasis
Purpose:	Improve individual skills
Total number of players:	3 players
Participating players:	Goalie
Training location:	Any
Spatial awareness:	Penalty box
Duration:	10-15 min
Physical skills:	Power & Speed

Organization:
Nine to twelve obstacles (alternative: stanchion with standing foot) are placed 6 m in front of the goal. The goalkeepers stand in the goal, the goalkeeper coach stands 11-16 m in front or next to the goal with the balls. The balls are deflected off the obstacles according to the height and accuracy of the shot so that the goalkeeper is forced to react quickly due to the ball's change of direction.

Equipment:
1 full-size goal, 2 small goals, 9 poles

Notes:
- The goalkeeper has to anticipate the ball's path at short notice. This trains his reaction speed.
- If possible the balls should be caught, if this is not possible he should push the ball off to the side.
- Just before the coach makes contact with the ball the goalkeeper performs a short, forward two-legged preparatory jump, or takes a short step forwards. He spreads his arms, bends his legs slightly and stands on the balls of his feet. The feet point in the direction of the coach and are around hip-distance apart. The torso is bent slightly forward and the eyes are fixed on the ball.
- Correct technique for the balls of the feet is important here in order to be able to push up quickly and firmly off the ground.

Field size:
Penalty area

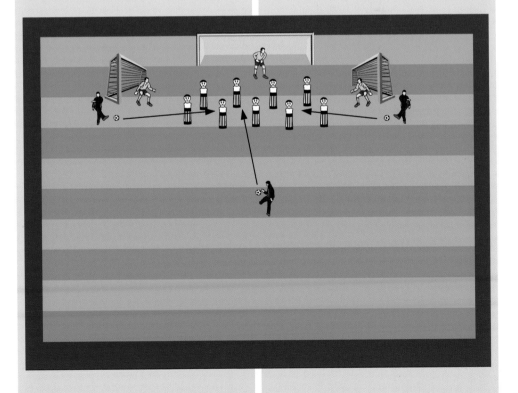

Training Target
- Goalkeepers

Training Emphasis
- Explosiveness
- Reactions
- Leaping power

Training Aspects

Skills involved:	Leaping strength, Quick anticipation, Flexibility, Speed of movement off the ball, Quick decisions, Quick processing, Quickness of reaction, Speed in change of direction, Quick understanding of danger
Age level:	Any age
Level of play:	Recreational
Type of training:	Individual training,
Training structure:	Small group training (2-6 players)
Purpose:	Improve individual skills
Total number of players:	2 or more players, Single player
Participating players:	Goalie
Training location:	Any
Spatial awareness:	Penalty box
Duration:	10-15 min
Physical skills:	Soccer-specific endurance, Power & Speed

Organization:
The goalkeeper stands at the near post according to the diagram. A goalkeeping coach (A) stands with the ball behind the goal, another stands 10 meters to the side (C) and another stands 10-12 meters centrally, in front of the goal (B). The balls are with the goalkeeping coaches.

Implementation:
The goalkeeper stands in the goal with his back to the open field. As soon as A drops the ball, the goalkeeper turns to face coach B whose first shot he tries to stop (towards the far post). He then immediately tries to stop the second shot from C, who aims for the near post.

Intensity:
6-8 repetitions

Order of movements:
A – Coach drops the ball
1 – Goalkeeper reacts to this signal, turns and tries to stop the ball from B
C – Second shot
2 – Goalkeeper's jump/reaction to the second ball

Equipment:
1 full-size goal

Notes:
- As soon as the coach starts to turn, the coach takes his shot.
- The goalkeeper tries to catch the balls, if this is not possible, he should push the ball off to the side.
- The take-off takes place either with or without an intermediate step. Taking many steps, wastes time. When taking off, the bodyweight is on the push-off leg.

- The goalkeeper jumps with momentum to the side. To the right, he laterally pushes off over the soccer ball. To the left, he uses his momentum over the left foot.
- The goalkeeper has a movement to the right and one to the left.
- Change the side and angle of the shots.

Field size:
20 x 20 m

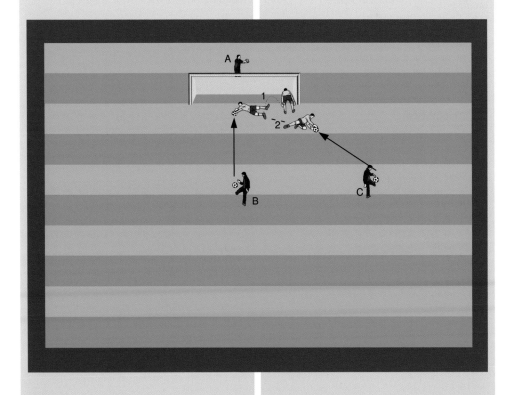

Training Target
- **Goalkeepers**

Training Emphasis
- **Explosiveness**
- **Reactions**
- **Leaping power**

Training Aspects	
Skills involved:	**Leaping strength, Quick anticipation, Flexibility, Speed of movement off the ball, Quick decisions, Quick processing, Quickness of reaction, Speed in change of direction, Quick understanding of danger**
Age level:	**Any age**
Level of play:	**Recreational**
Type of training:	**Individual training, Small group training (2-6 players)**
Training structure:	**Main point/Emphasis**
Purpose:	**Improve individual skills**
Total number of players:	**2 or more players, Single player**
Participating players:	**Goalie**
Training location:	**Any**
Spatial awareness:	**Penalty box**
Duration:	**10-15 min**
Physical skills:	**Strength endurance, Power & Speed**

Organization:
The goalkeeper lies on the ground in front of the goal. The goalkeeper coach takes up his position on the penalty line.

Implementation:
The goalkeeper lies on his stomach facing the ground. The coach gives a call signal, upon which the goalkeeper has to react as fast as possible and jump towards the ball.

Intensity:
6-10 shots

Equipment:
1 full-size goal

Notes:
- When getting up briefly, use a hand to push up with; the other hand is ready to react. If he decides to stand up using his right leg, he first gets up with his right leg and then pushes up with his left. He then lies with his torso laterally to the left, and leans forward with both arms, stands up first with his right leg and then pushes off with the left.
- Foot/tip of the foot points towards the ball not forward.
- The goalkeeper jumps with momentum to the side. To the right, take momentum over your right foot and laterally push off over the soccer ball. To the left, take momentum over the left foot.
- In this course of movements, the hands and face point towards the shooter. As a general rule, try to catch the ball.

Field size:
Penalty area

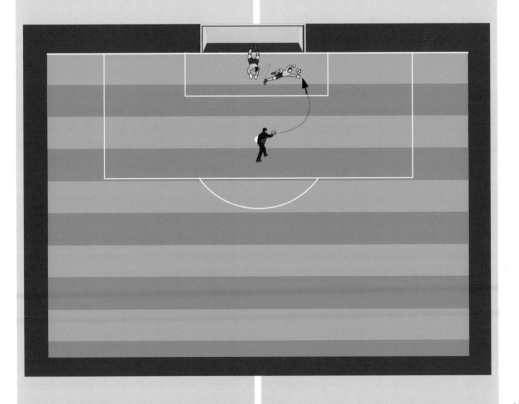

Training Target
- Goalkeepers

Training Emphasis
- Explosiveness
- Reactions

Training Aspects

Skills involved:	Leaping strength, Quick anticipation, Control, Flexibility, Speed of movement off the ball, Quick decisions, Quick processing, Quickness of reaction, Quick understanding of danger
Age level:	Any age
Level of play:	Recreational
Type of training:	Individual training, Small group training (2-6 players)
Training structure:	Main point/Emphasis
Purpose:	Improve individual skills
Total number of players:	4 players
Participating players:	Goalie
Training location:	Any
Duration:	10-15 min
Physical skills:	Soccer-specific endurance, Power & Speed

Organization:
The goalkeeper stands in the goal, 2 players position themselves in front of him on the 6-yard box. The goalkeeper coach stands between 10 and 16 meters in front of the goal. The coach has the balls.

Implementation:
The coach shoots from approximately 10-16 m in front of the goal. The two players obscure the goalkeeper's view of the ball without changing the direction of the ball. The goalkeeper has to react as quickly as possible.

Intensity:
Approximately 20 shots

Equipment:
1 full-size goal

Notes:
- This play is not easy for the goalkeeper, as he sees the ball very late, but the play represents a typical game situation.
- The goalkeeper tries to hold onto the ball. If this is not possible, he should push the ball off to the side.
- The take-off takes place either with or without an intermediate step. Taking many steps wastes time. When taking off, the bodyweight is on the push-off leg.
- The goalkeeper jumps with momentum step to the side. To the right, he uses his momentum over his right foot and laterally pushes off over the soccer ball. To the left, he uses his momentum over the left foot.

Field size:
Penalty area

Training Target
- Goalkeepers

Training Emphasis
- **Throws**
- **Passing**
- **Opening the field**
- **Positional play**

Training Aspects

Skills involved:	Leaping strength, Speed of movement with ball, Quick anticipation, Outside of the foot, Controlling the ball, Flexibility, Speed of movement off the ball, Quick decisions, Quick processing, Inside of the foot, Inside of the foot passing, Inside of the laces passing, Combining technical skill with movement, Long passing, Quickness of reaction, Laces, Quick understanding of danger, Advanced passing
Age level:	Any age
Level of play:	Advanced
Type of training:	Individual training, Small group training (2-6 players)
Training structure:	Warm-up, Progression
Purpose:	Improve individual skills
Total number of players:	3 players
Participating players:	Goalie
Training location:	Any
Spatial awareness:	Half-field
Duration:	10-30 min
Physical skills:	Soccer-specific endurance, Power & Speed

Organization:
A goalkeeper stands centrally 5-7 meters from the goal. The goalkeeper coach stands approximately 35 m from the goal on the left touch line, a farther coach or another goalkeeper stands the same distance away on the right touch line.

Implementation:
The coach plays a backpass to the goalkeeper (1). The goalkeeper controls the ball with his first touch. With his second, he passes the ball diagonally to the second goalkeeper or goalkeeper coach, who plays the ball back to the first goalkeeper coach.

Alternative:
The coach plays a high volley towards the goal. The goalkeeper catches the ball and throws it diagonally to his goalkeeping colleague.

Complete 8-10 repetitions each time.

Equipments:
1 full-size goal

Notes:
- Demand accuracy and a high pace over and over. Slow training does not develop game-winning skills.
- The standing leg should be positioned 30-40 cm laterally beside or in line with the ball.
- In the example of receiving and dribbling the ball with the right instep, the course of movements is so that the player controls the ball with the instep at the moment that it touches the ground. The leg is swung from right to left in the direction of the ball. The foot is led slightly from above to below in the direction of the ball (similar to the foot movement when

shooting on goal, but with a smaller back lift) thus stopping the ball from bouncing up and away. Here the bodyweight is completely on the left standing leg, the torso is twisted at the hips to the right (right shoulder is spun backwards). The sight is focused on the ball, and the torso is slightly brought over the ball.

- When receiving and dribbling the ball with the outside of the foot, the ankle is opened inward. The lower leg is bent inward at the knee so that there is movement of the foot from above to below and left to right in the direction of the ball. The contact area for the ball is the entire outside of the foot.

- The preferred passing technique for long (volleyed) passes is the instep: The ball is played partly wih the side foot and partly with the laces. The standing leg is positioned laterally next to the ball and the player's torso goes in a slanting position. The toes point down, similar to the foot positioning by laces. This passing technique has the advantage that the balls move with a higher speed and lower trajectory and hence forms a type of pass that is fast and easy to control (for the pass receiver).

- When performing a lateral throw out, the arm is stretched back like a javelin thrower, and the ball laid in the open hand. The outstretched arm is then powerfully thrown forward, just missing the ear. The bracing step is important here. When the goalkeeper throws with the right hand, the left leg is offset forward to the side, and vice versa when throwing with the left hand.

Field size:
Half-field

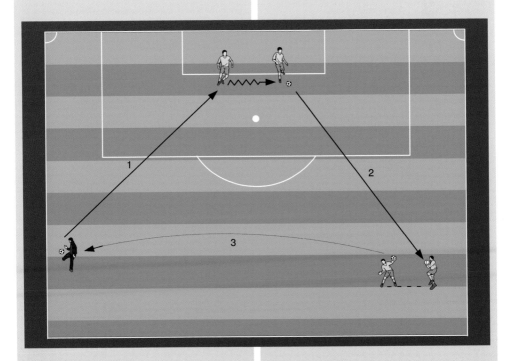

Training Target
- Goalkeepers

Training Emphasis
- Throws
- Passing
- Opening the field
- Reactions

Training Aspects	
Skills involved:	Leaping strength, Speed of movement with ball, Quick anticipation, Control, Flexibility, Speed of movement off the ball, Half-volley, Quick decisions, Quick processing, Combining technical skill with movement, Positional passing, Quickness of reaction, Opening the field from the goalie, Quick understanding of danger
Age level:	Any age
Level of play:	Advanced
Type of training:	Individual training, Small group training (2-6 players)
Training structure:	Main point/Emphasis
Purpose:	Improve individual skills
Total number of players:	2 or more players, Single player
Participating players:	Goalie
Training location:	Any
Spatial awareness:	Half-field
Duration:	20-40 min
Physical skills:	Soccer-specific endurance, Power & Speed

Organization:
Construct 3 goals according to the diagram. The two small goals are positioned to the left and right on the halfway line. The large goal is placed centrally on the touch line. The goalkeeper is in the goal. The goalkeeper coach stands approximately 12 m away with the balls.

Implementation:
The coach kicks the ball with a hard drop kick to the catching area of the goalkeeper. The goalkeeper catches the ball and plays it into either the left or right goal either as a drop kick or a throw.

Intensity:
20-30 repetitions

Order of Movements:
1 – Drop kick by the coach + ball catch by the goalkeeper
2 – Option: throw-out (goalkeeper)
3 – Option: drop kick (goalkeeper)

Equipment:
1 full-size Goal, 2 small goals

Notes:
- The take-off takes place either with or without an intermediate step. Taking many steps wastes time. When taking off, the bodyweight is on the push-off leg. The goalkeeper tries to hold onto the ball.
- When performing a lateral throw out, the arm is stretched back like a javelin thrower, and the ball is laid in the open hand. The outstretched arm is then powerfully thrown forward, just missing

the ear. The bracing step is important here. When the goalkeeper throws with the right hand, the left leg is offset forward to the side, and vice versa when throwing with the left hand.

- You can practice throwing techniques against a net, and afterwards incorporate the throwing action into shooting practice, in that after a ball is held, it has to be thrown into one of the goals built on the field.
- When performing a drop kick, take the ball in both hands, stretch out the arms and drop the ball. The ball has to be met with the laces at the moment it hits the ground. After contact, the leg follows through. The ball should not spin.

Field size:
Half field

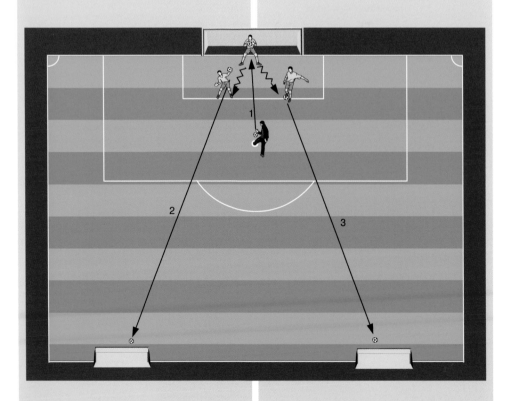

Training Target
- **Goalkeepers**

Training Emphasis
- **Opening the field**

Training Aspects	
Skills involved:	Leaping strength, Speed of movement with ball, Quick anticipation, Controlling the ball, Control, Speed of movement off the ball, Half-volley, Quick decisions, Inside of the laces passing, Passing over multiple stations, Quickness of reaction, Opening the field from the goalie, Laces, Quick understanding of danger
Age level:	13-14 years, 15 years to Adult, any age
Level of play:	Advanced
Type of training:	Team training
Training structure:	Main point/Emphasis
Purpose:	Offensive behaviors, Goalkeeper behaviors, Improve individual skills
Total number of players:	13 or more players
Participating players:	Whole team
Training location:	Any, Asphalt, Turf field, Grass field
Spatial awareness:	Half-field
Duration:	10-20 min
Physical skills:	Soccer-specific endurance, Power & Speed
Goalkeeper:	1 goalie

Organization:
Two 8 x 8 meter squares are built in line with the penalty area on the flanks (left and right). Two more are built on the flanks 35 meters away. One is also in the center of the field in line with the penalty area and one on the semicircle on the halfway line. The goalkeeper goes in the goal and in each square 2 outfield players position themselves (see diagram).

Implementation:
Two players stand in each square. One player receives the ball, the other passes it on.

The sequence:
A1 passes to the goalkeeper, who plays a long ball to A3, who kicks it to A4. A4 now plays a long ball to A2. B1 passes to the goalkeeper, who throws a long ball to B3, who kicks it to B4. B4 then plays a long ball to B2. C1 passes to the goalkeeper, who plays a drop kick to C3, who kicks it to C4. C4 then finally passes a long ball to C2.

Passes:
1. A1 passes to the goalkeeper.
2. After the goalkeeper's pass to A3, B1 starts his pass to the goalkeeper.
3. After the goalkeeper's pass to B3, C1 starts his pass to the goalkeeper.
4. After the goalkeeper's pass to C3, A1 starts his pass to the goalkeeper, etc.

Equipment:
1 full-size goal, 24 cones.

Notes:

- Precise passing.

- Communicate with each other. Help each other and call for the ball.

- The goalkeeper can decide whether he plays the ball by throwing, rolling, goal kick, clearance or pass.

- With this type of play, a game appropriate play-opening for the goalkeeper is studied.

- Laces: The tip of the foot points down, the ankle is tensed and the torso is bent slightly over the ball. The contact area is the area behind the heel. In order to achieve distance on the ball, a slight back lift is permitted.

- Side foot: The ball will be played partly with the side foot and partly with laces. The standing leg is positioned to the side next to the ball and the player's torso moves into a slanted position. The toes point down, similar to the foot positioning of the laces shot.

- Clearance technique (drop kick) When performing a drop kick, contact with the ball is made with the laces at exactly the moment that it hits the ground.

- When performing a frontal volley, the torso is bent slightly over the ball. The ball is thrown slightly forward and met at a low point. This way the ball receives strong pressure and a high degree of accuracy. The area of contact is the laces. In order to gain greater distance, position the torso upright or lean backwards slightly.

- When performing a volley from the side, the standing leg is positioned laterally next to the ball and the player's torso is angled. The toes point down, similar to a shot with the laces. The point of contact is the laces, the shooting leg is tilted at an angle and the ball is lightly guided or thrown by the hand to the shooting leg.

- When performing a lateral throw out, the arm is stretched back like a javelin thrower, and ball is laid in the open hand. The outstretched arm is then powerfully thrown forward, just missing the ear. The bracing step is important here. When the goalkeeper throws with the right hand, the left leg is offset forward to the side, and vice versa when throwing with the left hand. You can practice throwing techniques against a net, and afterwards incorporate the throwing action into shooting practice, in that after a ball is held, it has to be thrown into one of the goals built on the field.

- When rolling the ball, the goalkeeper places the ball in his palm, the leg closest to the ball steps forward and both legs are bent (crouched position). When rolling with the right arm, the left leg is accordingly placed in front of the right. At the same time, the bodyweight is placed on the left leg. The right arm is guided powerfully forward toward the ground and the ball is then placed on the ground. The hand thrusts the ball forward and determines the direction. The left arm makes an exactly opposite backswing movement, parallel to the left hand's rolling movement. The torso is bent slightly forward.

- The receiving and dribbling of the ball can either occur with the inside or outside of the left or right foot.

- With high passes/backpasses the ball has to be brought under control at the moment it touches the ground. If carried out correctly, the ball does not jump off the ground and can therefore be carried directly.

- In order to prevent the ball from bouncing up and to guarantee fast and fluid reception and dribbling of the ball, the goalkeeper has to have at his command good timing and the correct ball processing techniques.

- In the example of receiving the ball and dribbling with the right instep, the motion sequence goes like this: the goalkeeper has to take the ball with the inside of the foot at the moment that it hits the ground. In addition, the leg is swung from right to left in the direction of the ball. The foot is lightly guided from top to bottom in the direction of the ball (similarly to the foot movement for a shot at goal, only with a shorter backswing) and this prevents the ball from jumping up. Bodyweight is solely on the left standing leg. The bodyweight is shifted to the right through the hips (right shoulder is turned back). The focus is on the ball, whereby the torso is additionally brought slightly over the ball.

- When receiving and dribbling with the outside of the foot, the ankle is tilted inside. The lower leg is bent inward at the knee so that the foot movement from top to bottom and left to right in the direction of the ball can ensue. The area of contact is the complete outside of the foot.

Field size:
Half field

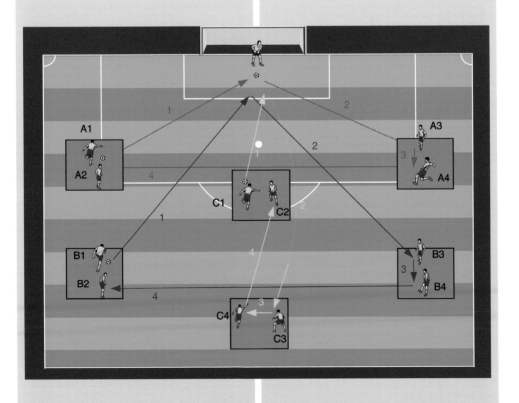

Training Target
- Goalkeepers

Training Emphasis
- Tactical drills
- Positional play

Training Aspects

Skills involved:	Defensive/Offensive play, Speed of movement with ball, Quick anticipation, Control, Speed of movement off the ball, Dribbling, Half-volley, Quick decisions, Quick processing, Inside of the foot passing, Inside of the laces passing, Combining technical skill with movement, Passing over multiple stations, Quickness of reaction, Opening the field from the goalie, Transitional play (shifting the game), Pushing, Quick understanding of danger, Taking on multiple players
Age level:	13-14 years, 15 years to Adult, any age
Level of play:	Advanced
Type of training:	Team training
Training structure:	Main point/Emphasis
Purpose:	Defensive behaviors, Cooperation within the team, Offensive behaviors, Improve individual skills
Total number of players:	13 or more players
Participating players:	Goalie
Training location:	Any
Duration:	10-20 min
Physical skills:	Soccer-specific endurance, Training of elementary endurance II, Power & Speed
Goalkeeper:	1 goalie

Organization:
A red and blue player position themselves on the flanks (left and right) in line with the edge of the penalty area, 35 m from goal on the flanks as well as in line with the penalty area in the center of the field and on the semicircle on the halfway line. The goalkeeper goes in goal.

Implementation:
The first ball is played to the goalkeeper from one of the 6 red players. In this case, from the right sided defender (right full back). The next player to whom the goalkeeper plays the ball is the left full back, whose opponent (A4) leaves the field. Now the 6 red players and the goalkeeper play against 5 blue players. The 6 players (taking the goalkeeper into account) have the task of holding onto the ball and keeping it in the opposition half. The weaker team of 5 players adjusts and tries to stop this and accordingly tries to attain possession of the ball and make a quick shot at the goal.

Equipment:
1 full-size goal

Notes:
- Fast, precise play opening.
- The red team always has the option to restart play through the goalkeeper when a forward pass is not possible.
- When in open spaces, use fast passing or ground-gaining dribbling.
- By directing the play down the flanks, the blue team tries to put their opponents under pressure and gain possession.
- Highly running intensive.
- Switching play, build up and pressing are studied alongside the goalkeeper's game-relevant play opening.

Field size:
Half field

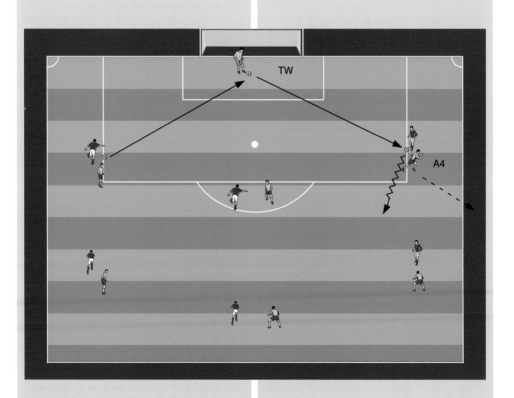

Training Target
- Goalkeepers
- Game system

Training Emphasis
- Opening the field
- Tactical drills

Training Aspects

Skills involved:	Speed of movement with ball, Quick anticipation, Control, Speed of movement off the ball, Dribbling, Half-volley, Quick decisions, Quick processing, Inside of the foot passing, Inside of the laces passing, Combining technical skill with movement, Passing over multiple stations, Quickness of reaction, Speed in change of direction, Opening the field from the goalie, Transitional play (shifting the game), Man down/Man up, Pushing, Quick understanding of danger, Taking on multiple players
Age level:	Any age
Level of play:	Advanced
Type of training:	Individual training, Team training
Training structure:	Main point/Emphasis
Purpose:	Defensive behaviors, Offensive behaviors, Improve individual skills
Total number of players:	13 or more players
Participating players:	Whole team
Training location:	Asphalt, Turf field, Grass field
Spatial awareness:	Half-field
Duration:	10-15 min
Physical skills:	Soccer-specific endurance, Power & Speed
Goalkeeper:	1 goalie

Organization:
A red and blue player position themselves on the flanks (left and right) in line with the edge of the penalty area, 35m from goal on the flanks as well as in line with the penalty area in center of the field and on the semicircle on the halfway line. The goalkeeper goes in the goal.

Implementation:
The first ball is played by the goalkeeper. The opponent of the player who receives the ball leaves the field (here A4). Now 6 + goalkeeper play against 5. The 6 players (taking the goalkeeper into account) have the task of holding onto the ball and keeping it in the opposition half. The weaker team of 5 players adjusts and tries to stop this and accordingly tries to attain possession of the ball and make a quick shot at the goal.

Variations:
- 6 + goalkeeper vs. 6 (Nobody goes out)
- 4 + goalkeeper vs. 6
- 6 + goalkeeper vs. 8

Equipment:
1 full-size goal

Notes:
- Fast, precise play opening.
- The red team always has the option to restart play through the goalkeeper when a forward pass is not possible.
- When in open spaces, use fast passing or ground gaining dribbling.
- By directing the play down the flanks, the blue team tries to put their opponents under pressure and to gain possession.
- Highly running intensive.
- Switching play: build up and pressing are studied alongside the the goalkeeper's game-relevant play opening.

Field size:
Half field

Training Target
- Goalkeepers

Training Emphasis
- **Trapping**
- **Passing**
- **Opening the field**
- **Positional play**

Training Aspects

Skills involved:	Leaping strength, Speed of movement with ball, Quick anticipation, Controlling the ball, Speed of movement off the ball, Quick decisions, Quick processing, Inside of the laces passing, Combining technical skill with movement, Long passing, Positional passing, Quickness of reaction, Opening the field from the goalie, Laces
Age level:	Any age
Level of play:	Advanced
Type of training:	Individual training, Group training
Training structure:	Warm-up, Progression, Main point/Emphasis
Purpose:	Improve individual skills
Total number of players:	2 or more players, Single player
Participating players:	Goalie
Training location:	Asphalt, Turf field, Grass field
Spatial awareness:	Half-field
Duration:	10-30 min
Physical skills:	Soccer-specific endurance, Power & Speed

Organization:
The goalkeeper stands 2-3 m from his goal. Approximately 6 m to the side of him stand the 3 goalkeeper coaches with the balls. Two small goals are constructed on the left and right side of the halfway line.

Implementation:
The goalkeeper coach throws a ball to the goalkeeper at chest height. The goalkeeper has to process this ball as fast as possible (catch or use his chest) and play it to the goal either on the left or right side on the halfway line. It is important to keep switching between left and right feet.

Intensity:
30 Repetitions

Variations:
A – Receive ball on the chest + kick with the instep with left foot.
B – Catch ball with both hands + kick with the instep of the right foot.

Equipment:
1 full-size goal, 2 small goals

Notes:
- Demand accuracy and a high pace (slow training does not develop game-winning skills).
- The standing leg should be placed 30-40 cm next to and in line with the ball.
- When receiving the ball, turn the chest in the direction that the ball is going to be played.

- If the ball is caught, quickly turn to the side of the goal where the ball be played from.
- Laces shot: The front of the foot points down, the ankle is tensed and the torso is bent slightly over the ball. The contact area is the area behind the heel. In order to achieve greater distance, slightly lean back.
- Kick with the instep: The ball is played partly with the side foot and partly with the laces. The standing foot is positioned laterally next to the ball and the player's torso tilts forward. The toes point down, similar to the foot position in the laces shot.

Field size:
Half field

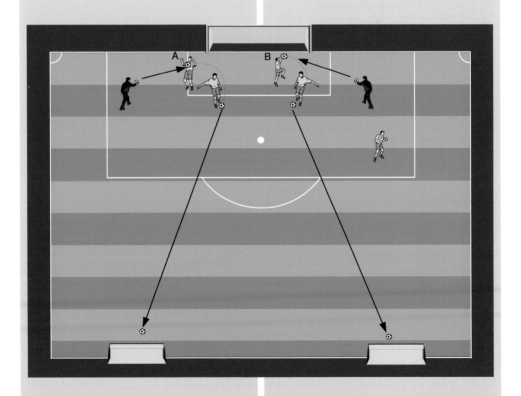

Training Target
- Goalkeepers

Training Emphasis
- Passing
- Opening the field

Training Aspects

Skills involved:	Leaping strength, Speed of movement with ball, Quick anticipation, Flexibility, Speed of movement off the ball, One touch passes, Quick decisions, Quick processing, Inside of the foot passing, Inside of the laces passing, Combining technical skill with movement, Long passing, Quickness of reaction, Opening the field from the goalie, Laces
Age level:	Any age
Level of play:	Advanced
Type of training:	Individual training, Small group training (2-6 players)
Training structure:	Conclusion, Progression, Main point/Emphasis
Purpose:	Improve individual skills
Total number of players:	2 or more players, Single player
Participating players:	Goalie
Training location:	Any
Spatial awareness:	Half-field
Duration:	10-20 min
Physical skills:	Soccer-specific endurance, Power & Speed

Organization:
The goalkeeper stands 2-3 m from his goal. Approximately 8-10 m in front of him stands the goalkeeper coach with the balls. One small goal is constructed in the center of the halfway line.

Implementation:
The coach plays a low back pass to the goalkeeper, who kicks the ball in the goal on the halfway line. The ball should be in the air when it reaches the goal.

Intensity:
Approximately 20 Passes

Equipment:
1 full-size goal, 1 small goal

Notes:
- Demand accuracy and a high pace (slow training does not develop game-winning skills).
- The standing leg should be placed 30-40 cm next to and in line with ball.
- Laces shot: The front of the foot points down, the ankle is tensed and torso is bent slightly over the ball. The contact area is the area behind the heel. In order to achieve greater distance, slightly lean back.
- Kick with the instep: The ball is played partly with the side foot and partly with the laces. The standing foot is positioned laterally next to the ball and the player's torso tilts forward. The toes point down, similar to the foot position in the laces shot.

- Instep shot or pass: The tip of foot points up, the ankle is tensed tightly and angled 90 degres to the side, the playing foot is slightly raised. The ball has to be met in the middle. Bring the body over the ball and avoid hunching the back.

Field size:
Half field

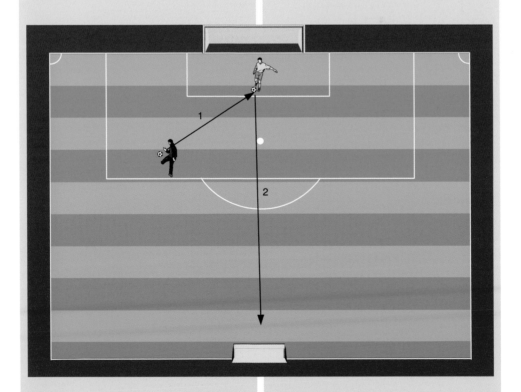

Training Target
- Goalkeepers

Training Emphasis
- Explosiveness
- Reactions

Training Aspects

Skills involved:	Leaping strength, Quick anticipation, Flexibility, Speed of movement off the ball, Quick decisions, Quick processing, Quickness of reaction, Quick understanding of danger
Age level:	Any age
Level of play:	Recreational
Type of training:	Individual training, Small group training (2-6 players)
Training structure:	Main point/Emphasis
Purpose:	Improve individual skills
Total number of players:	2 or more players, Single player
Participating players:	Goalie
Training location:	Any
Spatial awareness:	Penalty box
Duration:	10-15 min
Physical skills:	Soccer-specific endurance, Power & Speed

Organization:
A goalkeeper positions himself next to each post. The goalkeeper coaches position themselves 10 m to each side in accordance to the diagram.

Implementation:
The coaches play a firm placed shot on goal from a tight angle that the goalkeeper should save. The shots occur from left and right.

Intensity:
10-12 shots, then change sides

Equipment:
1 full-size goal

Notes:
- As a starting point, the goalkeeper is approximately an arm's length away from the post.
- Just before the shooter's contact with the ball, the goalkeeper makes a small jump forward with both legs, spreads his arms out wide, bends his knees, and stands up to the ball. The feet point towards the shooter and are approximately hip-width. The torso is leaned slightly forward and the eyes are fixed on the ball.
- The take-off takes place either with or without an intermediate step. Taking many steps wastes time. When taking off, the bodyweight is on the push-off leg.
- The goalkeeper falls with momentum to the side. To the right, by using momentum over his right foot, he laterally pushes off over the soccer ball. To the left, he uses momentum over the left foot.

- It is important for the goalkeeper to stay on his feet and cover his near post so that there are no little holes for the ball.
- The goalkeeper has to ensure that he does not let the ball bounce back into the center of the field; rather he should push it off to the side.

Field size:
Penalty area

Training Target
- Goalkeepers

Training Emphasis
- **Explosiveness**
- **Reactions**
- **Leaping power**

Training Aspects

Skills involved:	Leaping strength, Quick anticipation, Flexibility, Speed of movement off the ball, Quick decisions, Quick processing, Quickness of reaction, Quick understanding of danger
Age level:	Any age
Level of play:	Advanced
Type of training:	Group training
Training structure:	Main point/Emphasis
Purpose:	Improve individual skills
Total number of players:	2 or more players, Single player
Participating players:	2 Goalies
Training location:	Any
Spatial awareness:	Penalty box
Duration:	10-15 min
Physical skills:	Soccer-specific endurance, Power & Speed

Organization:
A goalkeeper positions himself in the center of the goal, and behind him there is a second goalkeeper. The goalkeeper coach positions himself centrally 10 m from the goal the with the balls.

Implementation:
The coach plays volleys alternating between the top left and right corners. The goalkeeper reacts as soon as he sees the coach shoots. One of the goalkeepers only reacts to shots in the top left corner; the other only reacts to shots in the top right corner.

Intensity:
6-8 repetitions, then change sides

Equipment:
1 full-size goal

Notes:
- It is important that the goalkeeper does not fall backwards. If he cannot hold onto the ball, he should push it away from the goal.
- Just before the shooters contact the ball, the goalkeeper makes a small jump forward with both legs, spreads his arms out wide, bends his knees, and stands up to the ball. The feet point towards the shooter and are approximately at hip-width. The torso is leaned slightly forward and the eyes are fixed on the ball.
- The take-off takes place either with or without an intermediate step. Taking many steps wastes time. When taking off, the bodyweight is on the push-off leg.
- The goalkeeper falls with momentum to the side. To the right, he uses momentum over his right foot, and laterally pushes off over the soccer ball. To the left, he uses momentum over the left foot.

Field size:
Penalty area

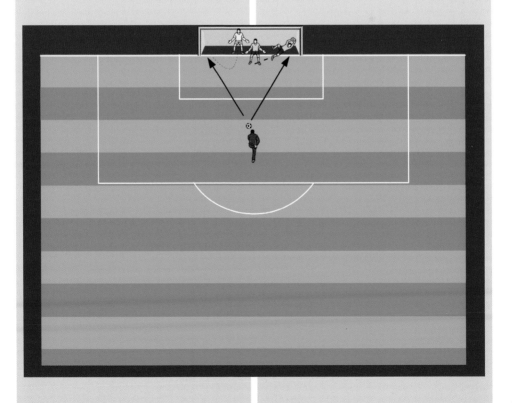

Training Target
- Goalkeepers

Training Emphasis
- Explosiveness
- Reactions

Training Aspects

Skills involved:	Quick anticipation, Flexibility, Speed of movement off the ball, Quick decisions, Quick processing, Quick understanding of danger
Age level:	Any age
Level of play:	Recreational
Type of training:	Individual training, Small group training (2-6 players)
Training structure:	Warm-up, Progression, Main point/Emphasis
Purpose:	Improve individual skills
Total number of players:	2 or more players, Single player
Participating players:	Goalie
Training location:	Any
Spatial awareness:	Penalty box
Duration:	5-10 min
Physical skills:	Soccer-specific endurance, Power & Speed

Organization:
A goalkeeper positions himself in the center of the goal, and behind him there is a second goalkeeper. The goalkeeper coach positions himself centrally 10m from goal with the balls.

Implementation:
The coach plays 15 hard shots one after another into the catching range of the goalkeeper. The goalkeeper's aim should be to fend off every ball and catch as many as possible.

Equipment:
1 full-size goal

Note:
- Just before the shooters contact the ball, the goalkeeper makes a small jump forward with both legs, spreads his arms out wide, bends his knees, and stands up to the ball. The feet point towards the shooter and are approximately hip-width. The torso is leaned slightly forward and the eyes are fixed on the ball.

Field size:
Penalty area

Training Target
- Goalkeepers

Training Emphasis
- **Explosiveness**
- **Reactions**
- **Leaping power**
- **Positional play**

Training Aspects

Skills involved:	Leaping strength, Quick anticipation, Flexibility, Speed of movement off the ball, Half-volley, Quick decisions, Quick processing, Combining technical skill with movement, Quickness of reaction, Quick understanding of danger
Age level:	Any age
Level of play:	Recreational
Type of training:	Individual training, Small group training (2-6 players)
Training structure:	Warm-up, Progression, Main point/Emphasis
Purpose:	Improve individual skills
Total number of players:	3 players, 4 or more players
Participating players:	Goalie
Training location:	Any
Spatial awareness:	Penalty box
Duration:	10-15 min
Physical skills:	Soccer-specific endurance, Power & Speed

Organization:
The goalkeeper positions himself in the center of the goal. The goalkeeper coach stands centrally 12 m from the goal. Two other players/goalkeepers/goalkeeper coaches stand the same distance away, albeit off-center. The balls are with the coach and the players are positioned to the side.

Implementation:
The coach and the two other players take turns shooting drop kicks at the goal. The goalkeeper stands in the goal and tries to stop the balls. It is important that he narrows the angle for each shooter accordingly, so that he repositions himself before each shot.

Intensity:
6-9 shots, then change. 3 rounds per goalkeeper.

Equipment:
1 full-Size goal

Notes:
- Just before the shooters make contact with the ball, the goalkeeper makes a small jump forward with both legs, spreads his arms out wide, bends his knees, and stands up to the ball. The feet point towards the shooter and are approximately hip-width. The torso is leaned slightly forward and the eyes are fixed on the ball.
- The take-off takes place either with or without an intermediate step. Taking many steps wastes time. When taking off, the bodyweight is on the push-off leg.
- The goalkeeper falls with momentum to the side. To the right, he uses momentum over his right foot, and laterally pushes off over the soccer ball. To the left, use momentum over the left foot.

- When performing a drop kick, the ball should be met with the laces at the moment that it hits the ground. Take the ball in both hands, stretch out the arms and drop the ball. The leg follows through after contact. The ball should not spin.

Field size:
Penalty area

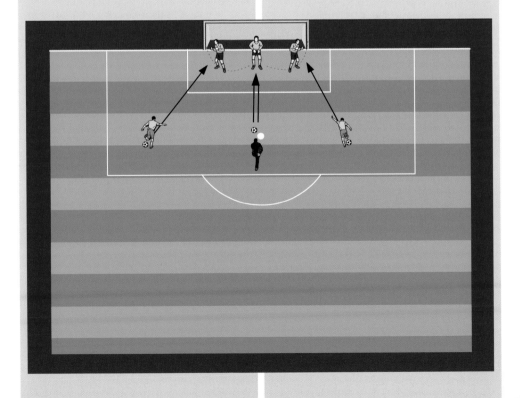

80 Dribbling from different starting positions

Training Target
- **Goalkeepers**
- **Activation/Warm-up**

Training Emphasis
- **Explosiveness**
- **Reactions**
- **One-on-One training**

Training Aspects

Skills involved:	Leaping strength, Quick anticipation, Flexibility, Speed of movement off the ball, Quick decisions, Quick processing, Quickness of reaction, Quick understanding of danger
Age level:	Any age
Level of play:	Recreational
Type of training:	Individual training, Small group training (2-6 players)
Training structure:	Main point/Emphasis
Purpose:	Improve individual skills
Total number of players:	2 or more players
Participating players:	Goalie
Training location:	Any
Spatial awareness:	Penalty box
Duration:	10-15 min
Physical skills:	Soccer-specific endurance, Power & Speed

Organization:
The goalkeeper stands in the goal. The goalkeeper coach stands 12-25 meters from the goal with a ball. After each turn, the goalkeeper coach starts from a new position (the diagram shows different possible positions for the coach).

Implementation:
The coach dribbles towards the goal and tries to play around the goalkeeper. The goalkeeper tries to use the one-on-one situation to his advantage.

Intensity:
6-8 rounds

Equipment:
1 goal

Notes:
- The goalkeeper should only pay attention to the ball and not react to the elusive actions of the coach.
- Remain standing upright for as long as possible, stretch arms out and keep feet shoulder-width apart.
- When quickly coming off your line, limit the attacker's angle. Just before the attack, slow down and move more gently on the balls of your feet.
- Don't spread your legs too far apart.
- The goalkeeper moves as quickly as possible to the center of the penalty area.

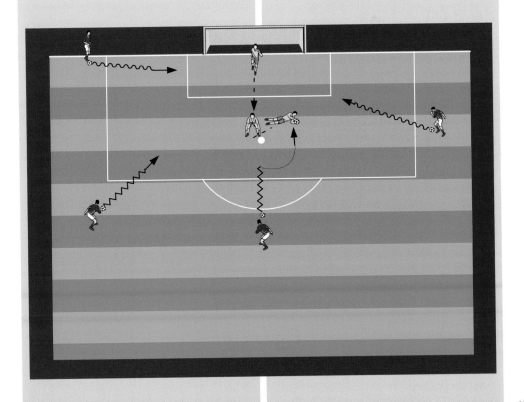

Training Target
- Goalkeepers

Training Emphasis
- One-on-one
- Explosiveness
- Reactions
- Positional play

Training Aspects

Skills involved:	Leaping strength, Quick anticipation, Flexibility, Speed of movement off the ball, Quick processing, Quickness of reaction, Speed in change of direction, Quick understanding of danger
Age level:	Any age
Level of play:	Recreational
Type of training:	Individual training, Small group training (2-6 players)
Training structure:	Conclusion, Main point/Emphasis
Purpose:	Improve individual skills
Total number of players:	3 or more players
Participating players:	Goalie
Training location:	Any
Spatial awareness:	Half-field
Duration:	10-15 min
Physical skills:	Soccer-specific endurance, Power & Speed

Organization:
The goalkeeper stands in the goal. Two players position themselves on the field as shown in the diagram. Player A stands between the penalty area and the side line and roughly 4-5 meters from the byline. Player B stands roughly 20-25 away from the center of the goal.

Implementation:
Player A dribbles to the baseline and passes the ball back to player B. Player B takes the ball and tries to dribble around the goalkeeper.

Intensity:
4-6 rounds, then change sides

Equipment:
1 goal

Notes:
- The goalkeeper must first concentrate on the passing player and determine whether the player will dribble to the goal, cross, pass or shoot. Depending on the action, he will have to reduce the shot angle but also keep an eye on the player in the middle of the field.
- The goalkeeper should try to be aware of just the ball and not react to the player's elusive actions.
- Remain standing upright for as long as possible, stretch arms out and keep feet shoulder-width apart.
- When coming off your line, quickly limit the attacker's angle. Just before the attack, slow down and move more gently on the balls of your feet.
- Don't spread your legs too far apart.
- The goalkeeper must only move as far as the penalty area.

Field size:
25 x 25 m

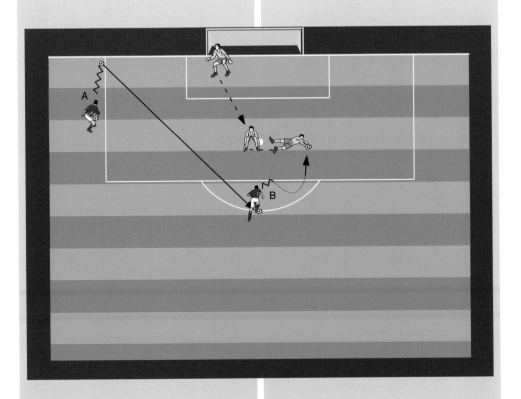

Training Target
- Goalkeepers

Training Emphasis
- **One-on-one**
- **Explosiveness**
- **Reactions**
- **Positional play**

Training Aspects

Skills involved:	Leaping strength, Quick anticipation, Flexibility, Speed of movement off the ball, Quick decisions, Quick processing, Quickness of reaction, Speed in change of direction, Quick understanding of danger
Age level:	Any age
Level of play:	Recreational
Type of training:	Individual training, Small group training (2-6 players)
Training structure:	Conclusion, Main point/Emphasis
Purpose:	Improve individual skills
Total number of players:	2 or more players
Participating players:	Goalie
Training location:	Any
Spatial awareness:	Half-field
Duration:	10-15 min
Physical skills:	Soccer-specific endurance, Power & Speed

Organization:
The goalkeeper stands in the goal and the goalkeeper coach stands in the dribble position with the ball between 12 and 25 meters away from the goal.

Implementation:
The goalkeeper lies on his stomach, looking at the ground. The coach dribbles the ball towards the goal and while doing so gives an initial charge toward the goalkeeper. As soon as the goalkeeper notices this, he stands up as quickly as possible and tries to win the one-on-one situation.

Equipment:
1 goal

Notes:
- The goalkeeper must pay full attention.
- When standing up, use one hand quickly to push yourself off the ground; the other hand is ready to react. If you choose your right leg, first stand on your right leg then push off the ground with the left. If your upper body leans to the left, support yourself by placing both arms out in front of you and then stand on your right leg and push yourself off the ground with your left leg.
- Don't point your foot and toes forward, but in the direction of the ball instead. The goalkeeper should try to be aware of just the ball and not react to the elusive actions of the coach. Furthermore, it's important that you don't run to the coach too quickly but instead stay as still as possible and reduce the shot angle for the player in possession of the ball.

- Remain standing upright for as long as possible, stretch arms out and keep feet shoulder-width apart.
- When quickly coming off your line, limit the attacker's angle. Just before the attack, slow down and move more gently on the balls of your feet.
- Don't spread your legs too far apart.
- The goalkeeper must only move as far as the penalty area.

Field size:
25 x 25 m

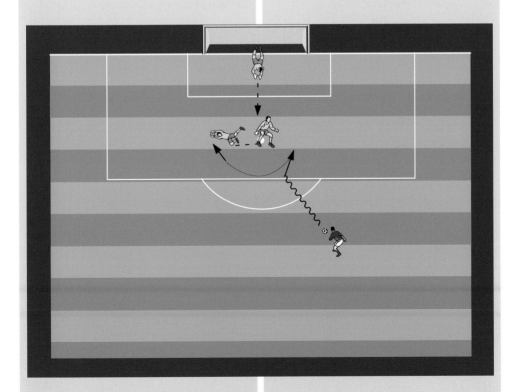

Training Target
- Goalkeepers

Training Emphasis
- Crossing/owning the box
- Leaping power
- Positional play

Training Aspects

Skills involved:	Leaping strength, Quick anticipation, Flexibility, Speed of movement off the ball, Quick decisions, Quick processing, Combining technical skill with movement, Quickness of reaction, Speed in change of direction, Quick understanding of danger
Age level:	Any age
Level of play:	Recreational
Type of training:	Individual training, Small group training (2-6 players)
Training structure:	Warm-up, Progression, Main point/Emphasis
Purpose:	Improve individual skills
Total number of players:	2 or more players, Single player
Participating players:	Goalie
Training location:	Any
Duration:	5-10 min
Physical skills:	Soccer-specific endurance, Power & Speed

Organization:
The goalkeeper stands in the goal. The goalkeeper coach stands about 6 meters away from the goalpost at the baseline with the balls.

Implementation:
The coach throws a high ball to the goalkeeper at the edge of the 6 yard box. The goalkeeper gets to the ball as quickly as possible and catches it at the highest point he can.

Repetitions:
5-6 repetitions then change sides.

Equipment:
1 goal

Notes:
- The ball should be caught at the highest point possible.
- Arms must be stretched out.
- Goalkeeper pushes off the ground with one leg and bends the other leg as protection.
- Bring the ball close to the chest as quickly as possible.
- Start by standing on the balls of your feet.
- Take small steps.
- The goalkeeper stands centrally, 1-2 meters from the goal and facing the ball.
- The legs remain parallel to each other and the knees should be bent slightly. Upper body should be bent slightly forward, arms remain at your sides and elbows slightly bent (stand like a cowboy who's just about to take his gun from its holster).
- To be able to guess the trajectory of the ball, the goalkeeper should only react after the ball has been shot.

- If he's unable to catch the ball, it should be punched away to the side with both fists (or one fist, if possible).
- To gain momentum the hand/fist dynamically moves up from behind and below to in front and above.

Field size:
16 x 16 m

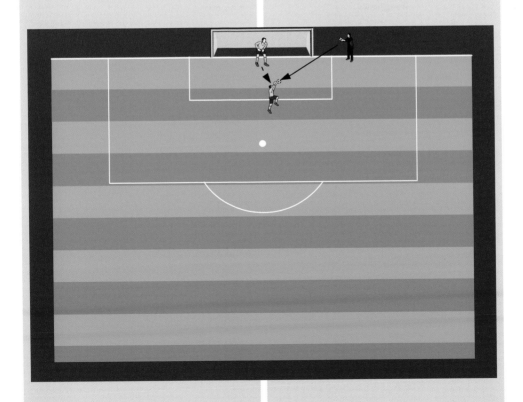

Training Target
- Goalkeepers

Training Emphasis
- Crossing/owning the box
- Leaping power
- Positional play

Training Aspects

Skills involved:	Leaping strength, Quick anticipation, Flexibility, Speed of movement off the ball, Quick decisions, Quick processing, Combining technical skill with movement, Quickness of reaction, Speed in change of direction, Quick understanding of danger
Age level:	Any age
Level of play:	Recreational
Type of training:	Individual training, Small group training (2-6 players)
Training structure:	Main point/Emphasis
Purpose:	Improve individual skills
Total number of players:	2 or more players
Participating players:	Goalie
Training location:	Any
Spatial awareness:	Limited playing field
Duration:	10-15 min
Physical skills:	Soccer-specific endurance, Power & Speed
Goalkeeper:	2-5 goalies

Organization:
The goalkeeper stands in the middle of the goal. The goalkeeper coach stands about 25 meters to the side of the goal in line with the 6-yard box with the balls.

Implementation:
The coach crosses a high ball in the direction of the 6-yard box. The goalkeeper tries to catch the cross at the highest point he can.

Intensity:
8-10 crosses, then change sides.

Equipment:
1 goal

Notes:
- The goalkeeper pushes off the leg farthest from the ball and pulls the other leg up near his body.
- The ball should be caught at the highest point possible.
- Arms must be stretched out.
- Goalkeeper pushes off the ground with one leg and bends the other leg.
- Bring the ball close to the chest as quickly as possible.
- Start by standing on the balls of your feet.
- Take small steps.
- The goalkeeper stands centrally, 1-2 meters from the goal and facing the ball.
- Legs remain parallel to each other and knees should be bent slightly. Upper body should be bent slightly forward, arms remain at your sides and elbows slightly bent (stand like a cowboy who's just about to take his gun from its holster).

- To be able to guess the trajectory of the ball, the goalkeeper should only react after the ball has been shot.
- If he's unable to catch the ball, it should be punched away to the side with both fists (or one fist, if possible).
- To gain momentum the hand/fist dynamically moves up from behind and below to in front and above.

Field size:
60 x 16 m

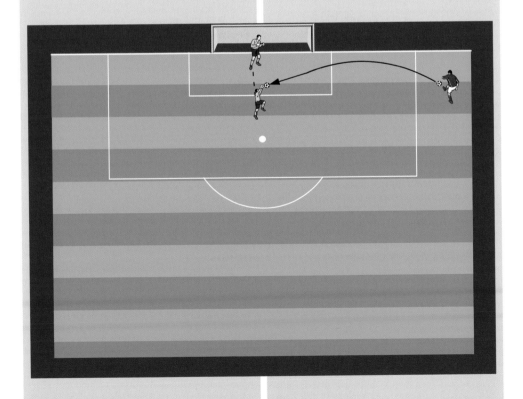

Training Target
- Goalkeepers

Training Emphasis
- One-on-one
- Crossing/owning the box
- Leaping power
- Positional play

Training Aspects

Skills involved:	Leaping strength, Defensive play, Speed of movement with ball, Quick anticipation, Flexibility, Speed of movement off the ball, Quick decisions, Bicycle kicks, Wing play without opponents, Quick processing, Inside of the laces passing, Combining technical skill with movement, Positional passing, Quickness of reaction, Speed in change of direction, Building an attack over the wings, Volley, Laces, Quick understanding of danger, Taking on multiple players, Advanced passing
Age level:	Any age
Level of play:	Recreational
Type of training:	Individual training, Small group training (2-6 players)
Training structure:	Main point/Emphasis
Purpose:	Defensive behaviors, Improve individual skills
Total number of players:	4 or more players
Participating players:	Goalie
Training location:	Any
Spatial awareness:	Limited playing field
Duration:	20-30 min
Physical skills:	Soccer-specific endurance, Power & Speed
Goalkeeper:	1 goalie

Organization:
The goalkeeper stands centrally, 1-2 meters from the goal. Two players position themselves centrally in front of the goal in line with the penalty area. Another player positions himself with the balls, as shown in the diagram, level with the side line.

Implementation:
The wing player makes a cross from the right (or left) side into the penalty area. Both strikers cross and try to finish the cross. The goalkeeper's aim is to catch as many crosses and let in as few goals as possible.

Intensity:
10-15 crosses per side

Equipment:
1 goal

Notes:
- The goalkeeper pushes off the leg farthest from the ball and pulls the other leg up near his body.
- The ball should be caught at the highest point possible.
- Arms must be stretched out.

- Goalkeeper pushes off the ground with one leg and bends the other leg.
- Bring the ball close to the chest as quickly as possible.
- Start by standing on the balls of your feet.
- Take small steps.
- The goalkeeper stands centrally, 1-2 meters from the goal and facing the ball.
- Legs remain parallel to each other and knees should be bent slightly. Upper body should be bent slightly forward, arms remain at your sides and elbows slightly bent (stand like a cowboy who's just about to take his gun from its holster).
- To be able to guess the trajectory of the ball, the goalkeeper should only react after the ball has been shot.

- If he's unable to catch the ball, it should be punched away to the side with both fists (or one fist, if possible).
- Decide whether he can get the ball or not.
- React quickly to connecting action (attacking players).
- The paths for both attackers are: the player at the back (from the perspective of the crosser) runs to the front post, the other behind in line with the back post.

Field size:
60 x 25 m

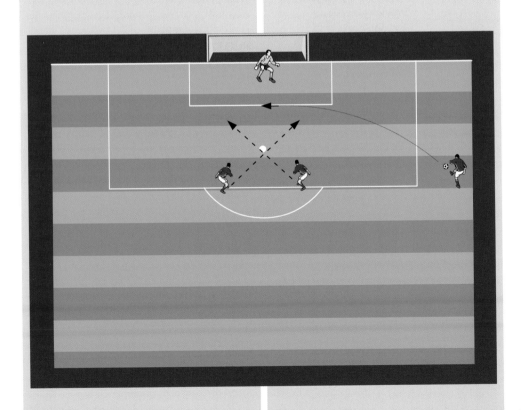

Training Target
- Goalkeepers
- Ball skill (touch on the ball)

Training Emphasis
- Explosiveness
- Reactions
- Leaping power
- Positional play
- Shooting

Training Aspects	
Skills involved:	Leaping strength, Speed of movement with ball, Quick anticipation, Outside of the foot, Trapping into space, Speed of movement off the ball, Wall passes, Quick decisions, Quick processing, Inside of the foot, Inside of the laces passing, Quickness of reaction, Laces, Quick understanding of danger, Advanced passing
Age level:	6-8 years, 9-12 years, Pee-wee (up to 6 years), Any age
Level of play:	Beginner, Recreational
Type of training:	Team training
Training structure:	Main point/Emphasis
Purpose:	Improve individual skills
Total number of players:	4 or more players
Participating players:	Whole team
Training location:	Any
Spatial awareness:	Limited playing field
Duration:	10-15 min
Physical skills:	Soccer-specific endurance, Power & Speed
Golakeeper:	1 goalie

Organization:
The goalkeeper stands in the goal. Position a starting cone. A rebounder positions himself next to the goal. The balls are with the players at the starting cone 16-22 meters away.

Implementation:
The player at the starting cone plays a pass to the rebounder standing next to the side of the goal and runs towards the goal. The rebounder passes the ball for the player to shoot on goal in a way that the player does not have to break his stride. Then the next player starts from the cone and the exercise is repeated. The rebounder changes regularly. The goalkeeper tries to stop the balls heading toward the goal.

Variations:
1. The starting player takes the ball with him and with his second touch takes a shot at goal.
2. The starting player plays a low or high pass.
3. The rebounder plays the ball back low or high.
4. In order to compete, count goals. The rebounder gets to follow up the shots on goal. In this variation, the rebounder can leave his position after he has played the ball back and actively follows up on the rebound.

Equipment:
1 full-size goal, 2 cones

Notes:
- The goalkeeper always takes his position based on the position of the shooter.
- Owing to the high variation of shots, the goalkeeper has to react differently to each different type of shot.
- The goalkeeper's aim is always to hold onto the ball.
- The goalkeeper acts as soon as the ball has left the shooter's foot.
- The takeoff takes place either with or without an intermediate step. Taking many steps wastes time. When taking off, the bodyweight is on the push-off leg.
- The goalkeeper jumps with momentum to the side. To the right, he uses momentum over his right foot, and laterally pushes off over the soccer ball. To the left, use momentum over the left foot.

- The outfield players' aim is to learn the correct techniques for instep-laces shot-volley and turning in order to increase the speed and accuracy of the shots.

Field size:
25 x 20 m

Placement of cones:
Goal-cone distance differs for age groups. Placement should be between 10-25 m.

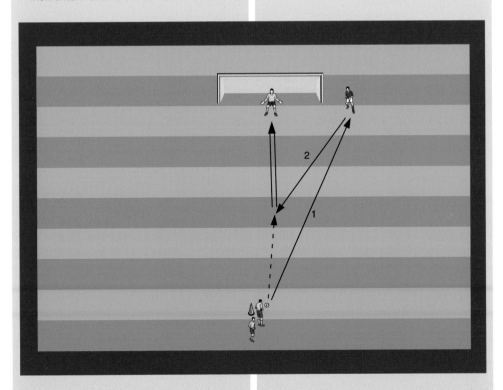

Training Target
- Goalkeepers

Training Emphasis
- Explosiveness
- Reactions
- Leaping power
- Positional play
- Shooting

Training Aspects

Skills involved:	Leaping strength, Speed of movement with ball, Quick anticipation, Outside of the foot, Speed of movement off the ball, Wall passes, Quick decisions, Quick processing, Inside of the foot, Inside of the laces passing, Quickness of reaction, Laces, Quick understanding of danger, Advanced passing
Age level:	Any age
Level of play:	Recreational
Type of training:	Group training, Team training
Training structure:	Main point/Emphasis
Purpose:	Improve individual skills
Total number of players:	4 or more players
Participating players:	Whole team
Training location:	Any
Spatial awareness:	Limited playing field
Duration:	10-15 min
Physical skills:	Soccer-specific endurance, Power & Speed
Goalkeeper:	1 goalie

Organization:
Construction of a starting and rebounding cone, in accordance with the diagram. A player is positioned at the rebounding cone, the other player(s) at the starting cone with the balls. The goalkeeper goes in the goal.

Implementation:
The starting player plays a double pass with the rebounder and dispatches his shot first.

Variations:
Shooting competition, count goals, or the rebounder can react to the rebounds.

Equipment:
1 full-size goal, 2 cones

Notes:
- The goalkeeper always takes his position based on the position of the shooter.
- Owing to the high variation of shots, the goalkeeper has to react differently to each different type of shot.
- The goalkeeper's aim is always to hold onto the ball.
- The goalkeeper acts as soon as the ball has left the shooter's foot.
- The take-off takes place either with or without an intermediate step. Taking many steps wastes time. When taking off, the bodyweight is on the push-off leg.
- The goalkeeper jumps with momentum to the side. To the right, he uses momentum over his right foot, and laterally pushes off over the soccer ball. To the left, use momentum over the left foot.

- The pass to the rebounder should be played with the strong foot.
- As soon as the starting player is in his starting position, the rebounder moves towards him and comes closer to the ball.
- The outfield players' aim is to learn the correct techniques for instep-laces shot-volley and turning in order to increase the speed and accuracy of the shots.

Field size:
10 x 25 m

Placement of cones:
Goal to cone B: 9-16 m
Goal to cone A: 16-25 m
Cone B to cone A: 7 m

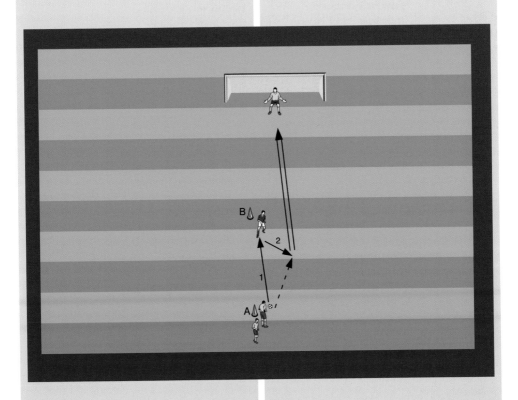

Training Target
- Goalkeepers

Training Emphasis
- Explosiveness
- Reactions
- Leaping power
- Positional play
- Shooting

Training Aspects

Skills involved:	Leaping strength, Speed of movement with ball, Quick anticipation, Outside of the foot, Trapping into space, Speed of movement off the ball, Dribbling, Quick decisions, Quick processing, Inside of the foot passing, Inside of the laces passing, Quickness of reaction, Direct play to the forwards, Laces, Quick understanding of danger, Advanced passing
Age level:	9-12 years, 13-14 years, 15 years to Adult
Level of play:	Advanced
Type of training:	Group training
Training structure:	Main point/Emphasis
Purpose:	Improve individual skills
Total number of players:	3 or more players
Participating players:	Whole team
Training location:	Any
Spatial awareness:	Limited playing field
Duration:	10-15 min
Physical skills:	Soccer-specific endurance, Speed endurance, Power & Speed
Goalkeeper:	1 goalie

Organization:
Construction of three poles and two starting cones in accordance with the diagram. The players divided themselves equally on the two cones. The balls are with Group A. The goalkeeper stands in the goal.

Implementation:
Player A dribbles from the starting cone towards the second cone. At the same time, player B starts his run to the pole. When they arrive, A plays a deep ball which B runs and dispatches at goal first, or after controlling the ball. Switch places after each round.

Equipment:
1 full-size goal, 3 poles

Notes:
- The goalkeeper always takes his position off the shooter.
- Owing to the high variation of shots, the goalkeeper has to react differently to each different shot technique.
- The goalkeeper's aim is always to hold onto the ball.
- The goalkeeper acts as soon as the ball has left the shooter's foot.
- The take-off takes place either with or without an intermediate step. Taking many steps wastes time. When taking off, the bodyweight is on the push-off leg.
- The goalkeeper jumps with momentum to the side. To the right, he uses momentum over his right foot, and laterally pushes off over the soccer ball. To the left, use momentum over the left foot.

- The outfield players' aim is to learn the correct techniques for instep-laces shot-volley and turning in order to increase the speed and accuracy of the shots.

Field size:
35 x 25 m or 35 x 25 m

Distance between cones:
Goal to poles: 25 m
Starting cone A to pole I: 6-8 m
Pole I to pole II: 12 m
Pole II to pole III 10 m
Starting cone B to pole III: 5 m

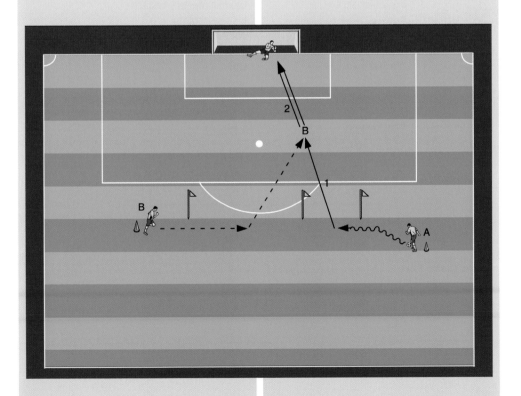

Training Target
- Goalkeepers
- Game systems

Training Emphasis
- Crossing/owning the box
- Tactical drills
- Positional play

Training Aspects

Skills involved:	Defensive/Offensive play, Speed of movement with ball, Quick anticipation, Control, Speed of movement off the ball, Dribbling, Half-volley, Quick decisions, Quick processing, Inside of the foot passing, Inside of the laces passing, Combining technical skill with movement, Header challenges, Passing over multiple stations, Quickness of reaction, Speed in change of direction, Opening the field from the goalie, Pushing, Quick understanding of danger, Taking on multiple players
Age level:	Any age
Level of play:	Recreational
Type of training:	Group training, Team training
Training structure:	Main point/Emphasis
Purpose:	Improve individual skills
Total number of players:	8 or more players
Participating players:	Whole team
Training location:	Any
Spatial awareness:	Limited playing field
Duration:	20-35 min
Physical skills:	Soccer-specific endurance, Training of elementary endurance II, Power & Speed
Goalkeeper:	2 goalies

Organization:
Each team splits up three players on the marked-out field. The goalkeeper takes up his position in the goal. The balls are located in the goals.

Implementation:
The two teams play 3 vs. 3 + goalkeepers. The aim for two minutes is to play at full speed and score or prevent goals. Afterwards, the outfield players are changed.

Equipment:
2 full-size goals, 6 cones

Notes:
- The two teams try to cover every facet of outfield player training.
- The goalkeepers continually organize their team.
- The play opening takes place depending on the situation (throw-in, side volley, etc.).
- Positional play is of huge importance.
- All the central themes of goalkeeper training are implemented (1 vs. 1, crosses, shots on goal, play-opening, etc.).

Field size:
32 x 32 m

Placement of cones:
Width: From goalpost to the width of the
penalty area.
Length: 16 m

Training Target
- **Goalkeepers**
- **Game systems**

Training Emphasis
- **Tactical drills**
- **Positional play**

Training Aspects

Skills involved:	Defensive/Offensive play, Speed of movement with ball, Quick anticipation, Control, Speed of movement off the ball, Quick decisions, Combining technical skill with movement, Header challenges, Passing over multiple stations, Quickness of reaction, Direct play to the forwards, Opening the field from the goalie, Building an attack over the wings, Quick understanding of danger, Taking on multiple players
Age level:	13-14 years, 15 years to Adult
Level of play:	Advanced
Type of training:	Team training
Training structure:	Main point/Emphasis
Purpose:	Improve individual skills
Total number of players:	12 players, 13 or more playersr
Participating players:	Whole team
Training location:	Asphalt, Turf field, Grass field
Spatial awareness:	Double penalty box
Duration:	15-30 min
Physical skills:	Soccer-specific endurance, Training of elementary endurance II, Power & Speed
Goalkeeper:	2 goalies

Organization:
A playing field of 2 penalty areas with two goals is constructed. The cones are placed in accordance with the diagram. In the center of each half of the field, three outfield players are positioned, as well as a player in touch (off the field) and a goalkeeper in the goal.

Implementation:
Two 5-man teams + goalkeeper take part. Three players on each team play with unlimited touches and one player on the wing. The defensive player is not allowed to tackle the winger in the "wing zone." The wingers are not allowed to leave their zone and should cross. The goalkeeper intensively participates in the play opening as well as goalkeeper-specific defensive action.

Equipment:
2 full-size goals, 12 cones

Notes:
- The two teams try to cover every facet of outfield player training, where the focus is on wing play.
- The goalkeepers continually organize their team.
- The the play opening takes place depending on the situation (throw-in, side volley, etc.).
- Positional play is of huge importance.

- This type of play often leads to action in the penalty areas, in which the goalkeeper requires fast reactions off the line, good positional play, the correct timing to intercept a cross and a swift precise play opening.
- All the central themes of goalkeeper training are implemented (1 vs. 1, crosses, shots on goal, play-opening etc.)

Field size:
Double Penalty Area
Alternatively the size of the field can be expanded to 40 x 40 m.

Placement of cones:
From goalpost to the first cone: 9 m.
Cone to cone: 5 m
Length: 16 m
When expanding the field, the distance between cones changes.

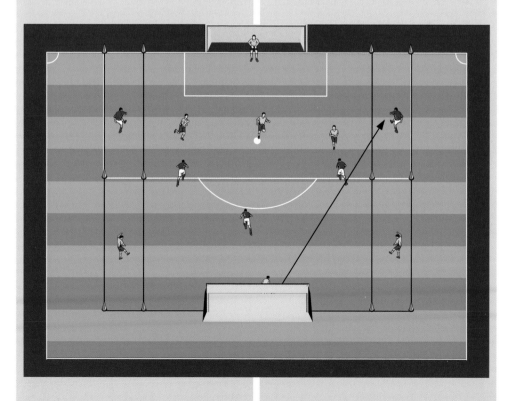

Many years ago the desire grew in me to put on paper and possibly publish all the knowledge and experience I gathered, first as a player and coach and later on during the internships, the coaching seminars and during the countless conversations with soccer enthusiasts. This book and the many others made it all come true.

I want to thank the following people and businesses:

Easy2Coach, who have given me new ways of showing the countless exercises graphically with their drawing software Easy2Coach Draw.

Together with the Meyer and Meyer publishing house I was able to publish my ideas world-wide and on various types of media (books, eBooks, numerous training packages as well as exercises in an online data base with integrated drawing and animation software).

Günter Limbach for his faith and his legal advice.

My father Johannes Titz, whom I could always count on, who has shown me my first steps in soccer and who never tired submitting more drawings of different exercises.

Meyer and Meyer publishing house and particularly Jürgen Meyer for the faith, the conviction and the helpful advice. Sebastian Stache, always by my side as a partner, a critic and a friend and who happens to be one of the best proofreaders any author could hope for.

My friend Prof. Dr. Steven Dooley who inspired me with his critical and constructive comments.

Thomas Dooley for his professional co-author ship and his faith in our coaching approach.

Timo Nagel, a friend and coaching colleague who stood by me for years with advice and support.

Finally I want to thank all the people who have supported me along this path and who have inspired my creativity. My family deserves the biggest thanks for taking the backseat all too often and for their relentless support throughout the entire process. Thank you!

Christian Titz